RAND NATIONAL SECURITY RESEARCH DIVISION

A Consensus Proposal for a REVISED REGIONAL ORDER in Post-Soviet Europe and Eurasia

CONTRIBUTORS

Samuel Charap, Jeremy Shapiro, Alexandra Dienes, Sergey Afontsev, Péter Balás, Rodica Crudu, James Dobbins, Vasyl Filipchuk, Diana Galoyan, Ulrich Kühn, Andrei Popov, Yauheni Preiherman, Pernille Rieker, Nikolai Silaev, Olesya Vartanyan, Andrei Zagorski

EDITORS

Samuel Charap, Jeremy Shapiro, John Drennan, Oleksandr Chalyi, Reinhard Krumm, Yulia Nikitina, Gwendolyn Sasse

Sponsored by
Carnegie Corporation of New York

For more information on this publication, visit www.rand.org/t/CF410

Library of Congress Cataloging-in-Publication Data is available for this publication.
ISBN: 978-1-9774-0361-2

Published by the RAND Corporation, Santa Monica, Calif.

Cover design by Rick Penn-Kraus
Cover image: Getty Images / erhui1979

Preface

Russia's relations with the West are in deep turmoil. This turmoil has manifested itself in various ways, including alleged Russian interference in U.S. and European elections, tit-for-tat diplomatic expulsions, and sanctions. These developments notwithstanding, the issue that originally sent the relationship off the rails and remains at the core of the broader dispute is the competition over Ukraine and the other *in-between* states: Belarus, Moldova, Georgia, Armenia, and Azerbaijan. This contest has become a negative-sum game, benefiting none of the parties: As a result, the West and Russia now find themselves locked in a dangerous and damaging competition, while the states of the region remain, to varying degrees, unstable, unreformed, and rife with conflict.

Despite the costs associated with the status quo, neither policymakers nor the expert community have proffered ideas about how to revise the regional order—in a manner that might plausibly be acceptable to all concerned states—to achieve stability, address conflicts, and facilitate greater prosperity. The poisonous atmosphere in relations among the key states has made an official discussion nearly impossible, and it is equally difficult for individual researchers to offer alternatives that take into account the range of complex and often conflicting national perspectives.

With support from Carnegie Corporation of New York and in partnership with the Regional Office for Cooperation and Peace in Europe of the Friedrich Ebert Stiftung, the RAND Corporation launched a project to fill this gap. To do so, we convened three representative working groups to devise alternative approaches to the three key elements of the dispute over the regional order: security architecture, economic integration, and regional conflicts. These groups of experts and former policy practitioners from the United States, the European Union, Russia, and the in-between states were tasked with finding mutually acceptable solutions to the current problems in these three domains. The results of their work are presented here.

This project was conducted in the International Security and Defense Policy Center (ISDP) of RAND's National Security Research Division (NSRD). For more information on the RAND International Security and Defense Policy Center, see www.rand.org/nsrd/ndri/centers/isdp or contact the director (contact information is provided on the webpage).

Contents

Figures and Tables

Figures

Tables

Acknowledgments

We are grateful to Carnegie Corporation of New York for its continuing support for this project in its current and earlier phases, and to the Friedrich Ebert Stiftung's Regional Office for Cooperation and Peace in Europe for its partnership. Additionally, we thank Lynn Davis and William Hill for their thorough reviews and helpful comments on the draft.

Abbreviations

CEPA	Comprehensive and Enhanced Partnership Agreement
CIS	Commonwealth of Independent States
CSBM	confidence- and security-building measure
CSTO	Collective Security Treaty Organization
DCFTA	Deep and Comprehensive Free Trade Area agreement
EAEU	Eurasian Economic Union
EU	European Union
EUMM	European Union Monitoring Mission in Georgia
FTA	free trade area agreement
IPRM	Incident Prevention and Response Mechanism
MSG	multilateral security guarantee
NATO	North Atlantic Treaty Organization
OSCE	Organization for Security and Co-operation in Europe
PKO	peacekeeping operation
PoC	point of contact
RSC	regional security consultations
SALW	small arms and light weapons
UN	United Nations
WTO	World Trade Organization

CHAPTER ONE

Introduction

Samuel Charap

At the core of the heightened tensions between Russia and the West is the contest for influence over the countries physically located between them (referred to here as the *in-between states*): first and foremost Ukraine, but also Belarus, Moldova, Georgia, Armenia, and Azerbaijan. While the relationship between Russia and the West was far from ideal before 2014, it was the Ukraine crisis that fundamentally changed that relationship, ruling out any remaining hopes for partnership and effectively institutionalizing a confrontational dynamic. The contest over the in-between states has taken a significant toll on these countries. The most extreme case is the war in Ukraine, in which over 13,000 people have died; other regional conflicts have occurred in Moldova, Georgia, and Azerbaijan, and the competition has also disrupted regional trade patterns and set back the process of reform and domestic transformation in these states. In short, all of the states involved—Russia, the countries of the West, and the in-between states—are less secure and prosperous as a result.

This dispute is fundamentally about the set of rules, norms, and institutions that govern the region: the regional order. The major powers (the European Union [EU], the United States, and Russia) have pursued policies toward the region that have contributed to today's disorder and instability. Despite these negative consequences, there is little indication that any of the states involved are prepared to rethink current approaches. In part, the absence of critical self-reflection is a consequence of the deterioration in relations among the states involved. However, the current stasis is also a function of the lack of new ideas and proposals to address the problem.[1] Indeed, the policy debate in the West regarding the regional order is usually a contest between advocates of further enlargement of Euro-Atlantic institutions (the EU and the North Atlantic Treaty Organization [NATO]) and critics of those institutions, who argue that enlargement caused the current crisis and should be halted.[2] This debate is increasingly divorced from the realities on the ground: For a variety of reasons, further enlargement to the in-between states is impossible today and will remain so, barring very low-probability exogenous shocks. Moreover, the in-between states are in no condition to qualify for membership, in part because of ongoing conflicts in the three most plausible membership aspirants; this includes a major war in Ukraine. However, the critics of further Euro-Atlantic enlargement are largely focused on *stopping* what they see as a misguided policy, rather than offering a coherent alternative approach that addresses the significant challenges in the region. Meanwhile, Russia has largely focused on resisting further enlargement of Euro-Atlantic institutions and consolidating its own existing alliances, while not putting forward an agenda that might change the ruinous regional dynamic. With the partial exception of Belarus, which has aired a proposal for a "Helsinki II" regional conference (a reference to the Helsinki Final Act of 1975), governments of the region have not advanced new ideas.[3]

In short, even though maintaining the status quo[4] will perpetuate instability in the region and a long-term Cold War–like atmosphere in West-Russia relations, the states involved seem likely to do just that if

---

[1] A partial and important exception is *Back to Diplomacy*, a report written by the Panel of Eminent Persons on European Security as a Common Project (Vienna: Organization for Security and Co-operation in Europe, 2015).

[2] See, for example: Luke Coffey, *NATO Membership for Georgia: In U.S. and European Interest*, Washington, D.C.: Heritage Foundation, Special Report No. 199, January 29, 2018; and John Mearsheimer, "Why the Ukraine Crisis Is the West's Fault," *Foreign Affairs*, Vol. 93, No. 5, September/October 2014.

[3] Artyom Shraibman, "Belarus, the Tactical Peacemaker," Carnegie Moscow Center, June 25, 2018.

[4] The term *status quo* is used throughout this volume to refer to the existing state of affairs; it does not imply that said state of affairs represents a stable equilibrium.

they do not develop a comprehensive and mutually acceptable alternative. This volume seeks to fill this intellectual void by outlining a revised regional order that would restrain the Russia-West contestation and boost the security and prosperity of the affected regional states. By *order*, we mean

> the body of rules, norms, and institutions that govern relations among the key players. . . . An order is a stable, structured pattern of relationships among states that involves some combination of parts, including emergent norms, rulemaking institutions, and international political organizations or regimes, among others.[5]

In this volume, we have broken down the concept of regional order into three components that are central to the dispute under examination: security architecture, economic integration, and regional conflicts.

Before describing our proposed alternative, it is important to establish the current state of the regional order. Today, the order in this region (see map in Figure 1.1) is dysfunctional. The security architecture is defined by the rivalry between NATO and its member states on the one hand, and Russia (along with the Russia-led Collective Security Treaty Organization) on the other. Armenia and Belarus are members of the latter, while Ukraine and Georgia aspire to NATO membership. Moldova and Azerbaijan remain nonaligned. But both blocs leave open the prospect of incorporating the in-between states, and thus all six are negatively affected by the contest among the major powers for their loyalty, including through the multiple wars of recent years. There is a similar situation regarding economic integration. Armenia and Belarus are part of the Eurasian Economic Union (EAEU), a Russia-led trading bloc with supranational decisionmaking on a range of external economic policy. Georgia, Moldova, and Ukraine have signed Deep and Comprehensive Free Trade Area (DCFTA) agreements with the EU, which, in addition to trade liberalization, provide for the incorpora-

---

[5] Michael J. Mazarr, Miranda Priebe, Andrew Radin, and Astrid Stuth Cevallos, *Understanding the Current International Order*, Santa Monica, Calif.: RAND Corporation, RR-1598-OSD, 2016.

Figure 1.1
Map of the Region

tion of current and future EU laws and rules into the domestic legislation of signatories.[6] (Azerbaijan, which mostly trades in hydrocarbons, remains unassociated with either bloc.) The EAEU and EU trading regimes are incompatible, and there is no regular dialogue between the respective commissions of the blocs. In-between states have been faced with an either-or dilemma, and economic ties between those states and one or the other bloc have degraded as a result. The long-standing negotiations for addressing the regional conflicts have been ongoing for years (in some cases, for decades) with only modest progress on conflict management and no prospects of achieving settlements. In large part, that has been a function of the interlinkage between the conflicts and other elements of the dispute over the regional order. Meanwhile, the panregional mechanisms designed to create order in all three arenas—e.g., the Organization for Security and Co-operation in Europe—have manifestly failed to achieve their mission and are largely deadlocked.

That is the state of the regional order today. Rival outside powers are pursuing mutually incompatible security and economic agendas that create binary choices for the states of the region. Conflicts, some hotter than others, have a deleterious impact on five of the six in-

---

[6] The DCFTAs are part of broader Association Agreements that cover a range of issues above and beyond economic ones, and EU integration itself is seen by a number of the relevant states as a geopolitical issue.

between states. These states have become a, if not *the*, primary battleground for the Russia-West competition, and this battleground seems to lack any functioning rules that might stabilize the contest. The dynamic has proven counterproductive for all parties, most of all the in-between states, which—in addition to direct security and economic consequences—are denied agency by the intensity of the Russia-West clash.

We recognize that the current tensions among the governments—as manifest in a range of disputes from alleged Russian interference in the 2016 U.S. presidential elections to the war raging in Ukraine's Donbas region—make negotiation of a revised regional order highly unlikely in the short term. Engaging in such talks would be a tremendously fraught endeavor—even in a better political climate—because they would touch upon subjects that have never been openly negotiated with both Russia and the Western powers at the table alongside the states of the region. Nonetheless, a window of opportunity could present itself in the future, since the status quo will only continue to deteriorate over time and therefore the associated costs might eventually prove too onerous for the affected states. This project was intended to provide ideas for decisionmakers about how to take advantage of such a window if it does appear. Furthermore, as noted previously, the lack of an understanding of what a mutually acceptable alternative to the status quo might look like is one of the reasons for the current stalemate and, therefore, describing such an alternative could help overcome the stalemate.

This volume offers a comprehensive proposal for revising the regional order. The detailed components of the proposal covering the three elements were devised by three groups of experts, convened by the RAND Corporation and the Friedrich Ebert Stiftung's Regional Office for Cooperation and Peace in Europe. All groups had representatives from the West, Russia, and the in-between states. The names of the participants are listed in the respective chapters to which they contributed. They each participated in a personal capacity and did not represent the views of their respective governments, but the groups attempted to take all relevant governments' interests into account. We further benefited from the input of a steering committee that provided guidance at the start of this process and feedback on early drafts of the proposals.[7] Each group had to make compromises to find common ground; the resulting proposals reflect that negotiation process and are thus unlikely to satisfy those who seek complete victory. Our objective in convening groups broadly representative of the key actors in this drama was to ensure that our proposals reflect the conditions of first-track multilateral negotiations with their inherently less-than-ideal outcomes.

It should be noted that, in addition to the proposals themselves, the language used in this volume reflects the process of finding consensus among authors with divergent views on fundamental questions, like borders. We therefore avoided using terms that implicitly endorse one or another national position on contentious issues.

The groups were given an unusual task. Rather than analyze current problems, or offer immediate policy recommendations, we asked the participants to focus on what would be desirable policies if there were sufficient political will to pursue a mutually acceptable alternative to the status quo. We deliberately avoided suggesting steps for policymakers to take in the current environment.[8] Instead, our proposal is geared toward a future window of opportunity. Therefore, by definition, the proposal contained in the following three chapters is not intended to be implemented today. However, it is nonetheless important for the broader policy communities in the affected states to consider because, if implemented, it would offer significant benefits for

---

[7] The group included Samuel Charap, senior political scientist, RAND Corporation; Reinhard Krumm, director, Regional Office for Cooperation and Peace in Europe, Friedrich Ebert Stiftung; Jeremy Shapiro, research director, European Council on Foreign Relations; Oleksandr Chalyi, president, Grant Thorton Ukraine; Gwedolyn Sasse, director, Centre for East European and International Studies, Berlin; Yulia Nikitina, associate professor, Moscow State Institute of International Relations; and a Polish participant who preferred to remain anonymous.

[8] That question was partially addressed in the publications of this project's first phase. Samuel Charap, Alyssa Demus, and Jeremy Shapiro, eds., *Getting Out from "In-Between": Perspectives on the Regional Order in Post-Soviet Europe and Eurasia*, Santa Monica, Calif.: RAND Corporation, CF-382-CC/SFDFA, 2018; and Samuel Charap, Jeremy Shapiro, and Alyssa Demus, *Rethinking the Regional Order for Post-Soviet Europe and Eurasia*, Santa Monica, Calif.: RAND Corporation, PE-297-CC/SFDFA, 2018.

all parties. The revised regional order would boost stability; facilitate increased prosperity; limit the major-power competition in the region, and thus stabilize the overall Russia-West competition; and better manage the long-standing conflicts in the region while increasing the chances of settling them. The revised order would thus limit the major-power confrontation in the region, stabilizing the overall competition between Russia and the West. Most importantly, the proposal would not cross any state's declared red lines, and thus might plausibly be acceptable to all of them. This is a vision for an alternative future that would represent a significant improvement, when compared with the status quo. The negative consequences of that status quo will only become more severe over time; therefore, it is likely that there will be greater incentive to rethink current approaches and begin talks in the future.

Indeed, the choice that all parties will eventually face is between a negotiated compromise and continued—and potentially more intense—instability. There are those in Russia, the in-between states, and the West who believe that a third option exists: Wait for the other side to collapse, implode, or dramatically weaken, and then impose their desired outcome. But, as the past several years have amply demonstrated, this approach guarantees instability and insecurity in the short term, with only the long-term hope of a highly unlikely contingency (the other side's implosion) producing a specific and anything-but-guaranteed outcome (imposition of preferences).

While the proposal contained in this volume might not provide recommendations that are actionable in the current political environment, it does offer a blueprint for a revision of the regional order that could be implemented when there is a window of opportunity for change. The next three chapters present the three elements of the proposal; the final chapter offers a summary of the entire proposal and a comparison between that proposal and the status quo. To implement the proposal, the current policies of all parties would have to change significantly. Again, this is highly unlikely in the short term. But, as the following chapters demonstrate, it is possible to conceive of an alternative that offers significant benefits to all. Current policy debates assume that no such alternatives—even long-term alternatives—exist;

this volume demonstrates that policymakers do have better options for the future.

Although the authors take direct responsibility only for the chapters to which they contributed, they and the steering committee had the opportunity to review the entire document and agreed to have their names associated with it. This entailed a process of finding consensus that was, at times, challenging. It should be noted that we were unable to reach a consensus regarding Crimea. Some participants, including those from Ukraine, argued that Crimea represents an issue that must be resolved in any negotiation on the regional order.[9] Others believe that in revising the regional order, all of the parties involved might have to agree, implicitly or explicitly, to set aside or shelve a few extremely difficult, contentious issues, such as Crimea—in effect, to agree to disagree on some important particulars while finding agreement on broader questions.

---

[9] One Ukrainian participant, Vasyl Filipchuk, specifically underscored his view that Ukraine's sovereignty over Crimea must be restored in the context of any negotiated revision of the regional order. See Vasyl Filipchuk, "What Should Be Ukraine's Position on Review of Regional Security Architecture," *Apostrophe*, August 28, 2019.

CHAPTER TWO

Regional Security Architecture

Jeremy Shapiro, James Dobbins, Yauheni Preiherman, Pernille Rieker, Andrei Zagorski

The current security architecture for the in-between states is not making those states, Russia, or the West more secure. Disputes surrounding the security architecture are at the core of the breakdown in relations between Russia and the West, and the architecture itself has failed to restrain the growing conflict. The result is that protracted conflicts have continued to go unresolved, new conflicts seem just over the horizon, and the in-between states are missing economic opportunities as the logic of confrontation undermines pragmatic cooperation.

The fundamental problem is that the current security architecture creates a binary choice for countries of the region. They can be loyal to one side or the other, but nonalignment seems a temporary option at best. Furthermore, any potential change in a country's orientation is seen as a loss for one side and a gain for the other. Such a bifurcation has essentially created competing, incompatible security architectures that render all parties less secure.

We propose a new understanding for a security architecture for the in-between states that would be accepted by all relevant parties and would limit the competition rather than precipitate security crises. Of course, the moment is hardly opportune for a such initiative—relations between Russia and the West have reached their lowest point since the end of the Cold War. But the status quo, left unchanged, will continue to perpetuate instability in the region and prevent cooperation, even on issues where there are shared interests.

Moreover, even if the politics did provide some small opening for progress, policymakers would not know how to take advantage of it.

Currently, both Russia and the West are much more focused on apportioning blame for the current instability than on devising compromises to improve stability. As a result, they have no vision for what a more balanced and inclusive security architecture would look like.

To fill this gap, this chapter proposes a revision of the regional security architecture that could be accepted by Russia, the West, and the in-between countries. This revision would not entail changing the current security institutions of Europe and Eurasia—for example, the North Atlantic Treaty Organization (NATO) and the Collective Security Treaty Organization (CSTO). We propose to start from where we are today. Transforming the existing institutions is neither a feasible nor a particularly desirable way forward. And while the early post–Cold War dream—of a common panregional security architecture from Vancouver to Vladivostok—might be appealing as a long-term objective to some, it is completely divorced from the realities on the ground and there is little practical policy guidance for how to reach that utopian future. We propose finding a way to build on the existing institutions, imperfect as they might be, in a manner that promotes stability.

The proposal consists of four parts. First, it proposes a consultation mechanism on the regional security architecture. Second, it describes norms that would define acceptable behavior for major powers, their smaller alliance partners, and other states of the region to prevent future misunderstandings and conflicts. Third, it proposes a *third way*: a set of arrangements that nonmembers of alliances could adopt that might be acceptable to all sides. These arrangements would provide security benefits to states that adopt them and would reduce the destabilizing competition between the West and Russia over nonmembers of alliances. Finally, it describes confidence- and security-building measures (CSBMs) that states could implement to provide a tangible manifestation of the new norms on the ground and provide some assurance that they would be observed.

This proposal would require Russia and the countries of the West to recognize that they gain little from persistent geopolitical competition over the in-between states. It would reflect an understanding that they can best satisfy their interest in security from each other by offering a mutually acceptable geopolitical status for these countries. (By geopolitical status, we mean the nature of a country's external security arrangements, including its relationship with political-military blocs.) In other words, for Russia and the West, mutual enhancement of the security of the in-between states is a means of creating security for themselves. Of course, if the true goal of either side is simply to build an ever-expanding bloc and to dominate the region completely, our proposal will not work. But even today there is little evidence that either side seeks that outcome.[1] If one side were to develop these ambitions, the architecture we propose would quickly expose them. The CSBMs would provide a mechanism to detect and demonstrate early indications of hostile intent, while the multilateral security guarantees would provide a standard by which to judge any violations. Today, the system that currently exists allows for significant ambiguity regarding objectives, and thus perpetuates insecurity.

The intent of our proposal is not to realize the early post–Cold War dreams of a Europe free of dividing lines. Rather, we seek to demonstrate that, even under conditions of continued competition between Russia and the West, it is possible to imagine a more balanced security architecture for this region that could contribute to stability, rather than encourage instability and conflict.

A revised security architecture cannot function effectively without solutions to the two other components of the regional order (economic integration and regional conflicts) highlighted in this volume. This is particularly true of the regional conflicts. It would be unreasonable to expect countries of the region to sign up to new security arrangements that ignore their primary security concerns (i.e., the conflicts). Accordingly, we assume that the solutions proposed in Chapters Three and Four will be negotiated in parallel to this revised architecture. Our proposal would not function without simultaneous progress on those issues. The nature of the linkage with the conflicts (and, to a lesser extent, economic issues) will vary for each in-between country, but the general principle is that a security superstructure cannot be agreed without parallel substantive steps forward on the concrete manifesta-

---

[1] Charap, Shapiro, and Demus, 2018, pp. 31–32.

tions of regional insecurity. An architectural plan cannot be realized if the building site is engulfed in flames. That said, it would be counterproductive to condition starting the process of creating a revised architecture on successful conclusions of the other talks; these processes and discussions must be pursued on simultaneous, parallel tracks. After all, the linkages go both ways: Progress on the security architecture is necessary to facilitate progress on the conflicts and economic integration pieces.

The remainder of this chapter proceeds as follows. First, we describe the current security arrangements of the in-between states. Second, we offer our three-part proposal for a revised security architecture. Finally, we demonstrate how the proposed system would function, using the example of a hypothetical change of government in Belarus.

The Status Quo and Its Shortcomings

Competition among the major powers is the main cause of the dysfunction in the current regional security architecture, but the in-between states have borne the brunt of that dysfunction. They have experienced war, large-scale population dislocations, and lost economic opportunities. Accordingly, it is important to understand what the in-between states all want (and need) from a revised security architecture.[2]

Today, the in-between states have differing security arrangements and ambitions, though all are suffering—to varying degrees—from the shortcomings of the status quo. Every country of the region, in other words, is unhappy in its own way. Nonetheless, among the six countries, the following three categories present themselves:

---

[2] The contestation over alignments in Europe and Eurasia extends well beyond the six in-between states. Russia and the West engage in contests for countries' geopolitical loyalty in other subregions, like the Western Balkans. The competition is sharpest, however, in the in-between states. If a revised security architecture can reduce competition over geopolitical status and improve the stability of the in-between states, then it could prove applicable elsewhere.

1. **Nonaligned (Azerbaijan, Moldova):** Countries that want to maintain nonalignment vis-à-vis Russia and the West, and that pursue relations with both, even if they occasionally tilt in one direction or the other.[3] These countries fear being forced to choose and want an architecture that allows them to pursue their own security policy, free from pressure to participate in the confrontation among the major powers.
2. **Russian-allied (Armenia, Belarus):** Countries that have a defense alliance with Russia and are interested in preserving it, but that at the same time see a vital interest in stressing their own sovereignty. These countries want to avoid becoming a battlefield in the Russia-West conflict and want to have ties with the West without compromising their allied status.
3. **Western-leaning (Ukraine, Georgia):** Countries that seek—but have not achieved—alliance with the West. These countries want to find a place under the Western security umbrella that will allow them to settle their conflicts, preserve their independence free from Russian coercion or future aggression, and have constructive relations with their neighbors, including Russia, despite their aspirations for membership in NATO.

In different ways, the current architecture puts all of these states in a bind. It works for none of them. The nonaligned risk finding their status under pressure from both sides, since neither Russia nor the West has committed to supporting it. The Russian-allied states worry about total Russian domination, but cannot truly diversify their relations for fear that they will become the next battlefield if they do. The Western-leaning countries continue to seek NATO (and European Union [EU]) membership—despite having few prospects of ever obtaining it—because they cannot conceive of another way to ensure their own security. All three current approaches contribute, to varying degrees, to the Russia-West conflict, because they allow the major powers to use any of the in-between states as objects of contestation

---

[3] Moldova, as a signatory of an Association Agreement with the EU, is far more politically integrated with the West than Azerbaijan.

to gain geopolitical advantage. As a result, the in-between states are denied agency in determining their own futures no matter which of the three paths they choose.

Proposal

The revised architecture we propose seeks to allow differentiation in security arrangements to persist, recognizing that the six countries involved are quite distinct. At the same time, our proposal addresses the source of the problems associated with all three current approaches: the contestation of the states' geopolitical status by Russia and the West. Therefore, the first task of the architecture is to ensure that the status of the in-between states does not fuel destabilizing conflict between Russia and the West. Our proposal achieves that by making sure that any changes in the geopolitical status of the in-between states proceed through a mutually agreed process that involves all the relevant powers.

The proposal for a revised architecture takes the needs of the in-between states into account while also providing confidence to the major powers that the system cannot be abused for any single party's advantage. Most importantly, it seeks to establish a process in which future changes in geopolitical status could occur without fundamentally upsetting the system and creating conflict. It would work through four interlocking components: (1) a new regional mechanism for consultation, (2) a commitment to norms that govern behavior, (3) a defined nonaligned status for in-between states (the third way), and (4) a package of multilateral security guarantees (MSGs) and accompanying CSBMs for those states that adopt the status.

Regional Security Consultations

We propose to establish regular consultations (outside of existing institutions) to discuss the regional security architecture and address any disputes regarding it and provide mutual reassurance about intentions. These consultations would not entail the creation of a new formal institution or be tied directly to existing institutions such as the Organization for Security and Co-operation in Europe (OSCE). Instead, like many standing multilateral consultations, such as the Global Coalition to Defeat the Islamic State in Iraq and Syria, the regional security consultations (RSC) would entail regularly scheduled meetings and ad hoc meetings as needed. The permanent participants in the RSC would be the United States, Russia, and the EU. However, any in-between state would have the right to participate at the regular meetings if issues relating to its interests are on the agenda. Any permanent participant or in-between state would have the right to convene an emergency meeting on potential changes to regional security arrangements or a crisis situation. Thus, no talks about a state would occur without its voice being heard.

Since these would be informal talks, any agreements reached in the context of the RSC would have no legal effect and would not be binding on other states. The general principles spelled out in the Helsinki Final Act would be the basis of the RSC's work, including (but not limited to) sovereign equality, refraining from the threat or use for force, the inviolability of frontiers, the territorial integrity of states, nonintervention in internal affairs, observance in good faith of obligations under international law, and respect for human rights.

The primary purpose of the RSC is to ensure regular major power consultation on the regional security architecture and to have a mechanism for crisis management surrounding potential future changes in the status of the in-between states. At the moment, one of the core sources of tension is the lack of discussion among the EU, the United States, and Russia on this issue. Furthermore, as we have seen in the case of Ukraine, there is no mechanism to allow for crisis consultations if an in-between state seeks (or is perceived to seek) a change in its status. The RSC would allow for such consultations.

Establishing the RSC will immediately raise concerns about the major powers' making decisions "over the heads" of the in-between states, or even allegations of a new Yalta agreement. That document, signed by Winston Churchill, Franklin D. Roosevelt, and Joseph Stalin at the end of World War II, has come to be seen as the epitome of great powers' imposition of their will on powerless third countries. However, the RSC will have nothing in common with Yalta. Its purpose is to ensure consultations, regular dialogue, and transparency, not to negotiate agreements like the Yalta accords. Any affected third states will have the right to convene the RSC and be heard, and no agreements will be made regarding any state without its participation. All states will remain free to seek membership in any international organization.[4]

Norms of Behavior

The RSC would function on the basis of two key norms of behavior. The central commitment for the permanent participants in the RSC is to try to achieve consensus among themselves before implementing changes to the regional security architecture. The participants would commit not to seek future changes in the composition of existing regional security institutions (i.e., growth in membership) or in the geopolitical status of current alliance members (i.e., undermining a bloc's unity) without mutual consultations, giving due weight to regional stability and the security interests of all parties. In other words, this would be a mutual commitment not to pursue institutional enlargement without consultation and attempts to find consensus and not to threaten existing institutions and their current memberships. The permanent participants would cease to pursue unilateral policies that are aimed at pulling states fully into their respective camps. This could be thought of as a norm of geopolitical nonpoaching. Since this is a political commitment, not a legal one, it would not preclude any state from joining any organization based on mutual consent.

The second norm concerns those in-between states that adopt the *third way* (see next section) status. Any state adopting that status would commit to consulting with the permanent participants if it chooses to change its security arrangements in the future.

A "Third Way": A Status Offer to Current (and Potentially Future) Nonmembers of Alliances

Currently nonaligned in-between states (Moldova and Azerbaijan) would receive an offer (which each state is free to reject if it so chooses) for a defined geopolitical status, accepted by both Russia and the West.

---

4 It should be noted that no OSCE or other document provides for the right to *join* international organizations (Charap, Shapiro, and Demus, 2018, pp. 27–31).

That status would ensure respect for the state's nonalignment, provide legally binding security guarantees, and preclude future major-power conflicts regarding its status in return for its agreement to seek changes in alignment only in consultation with the permanent participants of the RSC. To give practical effect to the major powers' commitments, the states that adopt this offer would receive MSGs and CSBMs (described in detail below) from those powers that will ensure that their nonaligned status is reflected in the military posture and activities of both rival blocs. The arrangement we propose is based on asymmetric pledges. Nonaligned states commit themselves not to take actions inconsistent with their status, while the major powers would commit themselves to respect that status as long as the nonaligned countries live up to their commitments.

Of the six countries examined here, this new status offer would only be immediately appropriate for the two nonmembers of alliances that do not aspire to such membership: Moldova and Azerbaijan. If these states were to accept the third-way status offer, it would enhance their security through an explicit recognition and endorsement of their nonaligned status by Russia, the EU and its member states, and the United States. It should be an attractive offer for existing nonaligned states because it makes both Russia and the West less of a threat to their independence. It would also make possible the enhanced measures for addressing protracted conflicts, which are described in Chapter Four. In return, those states would explicitly embrace their nonaligned status and commit to consult with the permanent members of the RSC on any future changes in their status.

The Western-leaning states would be free to continue their current course, but the prospects for achieving their aspirations would be just as dim as those prospects are today. But if the third-way status provided to the nonaligned states proved effective, that status may at some point become attractive for the Western-leaning states too. Moreover, embracing the third-way status would offer the best chance for these states to restore their territorial integrity, including through the measures outlined in Chapter Four. The least-safe option for an in-between state is seeking an alliance guarantee that is unlikely to be accorded, as this stance antagonizes one major power without gaining protection from the other.

The Russian-allied states could only obtain this third-way status offer by convening the permanent participants of the RSC and attempting to obtain their mutual consent. However, they would be better off under this proposal, even if they remain in the Russian camp; since the West would stop attempting to poach them, Moscow would stop trying to limit their relations with the West.

Beyond these six, this new status could also be adopted by OSCE participating states that are currently nonaligned (e.g., Serbia) or an alliance member that decides to exit its alliance in the future.

A Package of MSGs and CSBMs

For states that adopt the third way, the major powers will undertake measures—MSGs and CSBMs—that demonstrate commitment to their nonaligned status and provide reassurance to all sides that future changes in status will not be implemented unilaterally. These measures lie at the heart of the proposal and have a somewhat checkered past; therefore, it is worth describing in some detail how they can work.

MSGs: A Brief History

Security guarantees come in three basic forms. The first form is an *alliance*, in which several states guarantee to protect one another against a third party or parties that are usually unspecified but generally known.[5] The second form is a *collective security arrangement*, where all states guarantee to defend all states against aggression from any state. The most prominent historical example was the League of Nations. The third category is an MSG, whereby two or more competing powers mutually guarantee the security of a third state, usually on the understanding that the third country will not align with either power. Historically, these arrangements tended to occur when the third country was a minor power that physically separated two larger potential adversaries.

---

[5] Some alliances are nonreciprocal. For instance, the United States is committed by treaty to help defend Japan and South Korea, but Japan and South Korea are not committed to defend the United States.

None of these sorts of arrangements have unblemished records. Alliances lose wars as often as they win them.[6] Collective security works when the major powers with the capacity to provide for it agree and does not work when they do not. The third form of guarantee is not so much a commitment to support a state if it is threatened, but rather a promise of mutual restraint toward that state, whereby major powers pledge to respect the sovereignty of a smaller power if their rival (or rivals) do the same. MSGs are reciprocal, in the sense that the recipient commits to some behavior—in this case, nonalignment. The reliability of these arrangements generally depends on the durability of the equilibrium which gave rise to it. When those circumstances change, one major power or another may find an excuse to void the agreement.

MSGs have often resulted in the creation of a buffer state, one separating two potential adversaries while remaining unaligned with either. Rajan Menon and Jack L. Snyder's study of 12 prominent 19th- and 20th-century buffer states indicates that formal agreement among the buffer and buffered states is not in all cases required for success.[7] In addition, the buffer state must demonstrate certain qualities to ensure the success of the arrangement: competent governance, difficult physical terrain, the capacity to raise the costs to an intruder and, most importantly, internal cohesion around a coherent strategy for sustaining the buffer role. Menon and Snyder's research indicates that MSGs for in-between states, if they were to endure, would require not just Russian and Western agreement but also a clear embrace by those countries of their responsibility to maintain a balance between two competing alliance systems. In other words, MSGs are not simply granted by major powers; they must be accepted and embraced by the recipient states, or they are unlikely to function as intended.

The 1955 Austrian State Treaty is an example of a functioning MSG that provided benefits to both the guarantors and the guaranteed parties. Austria was occupied after World War II by the Western allies

---

6 Douglas M. Gibler, *International Military Alliances, 1648–2008*, Vol. 2, Washington, D.C.: CQ Press, 2009.

7 Rajan Menon and Jack L. Snyder, "Buffer Zones: Anachronism, Power Vacuum, or Confidence Builder?" *Review of International Studies*, Vol. 43, No. 5, December 2017.

and the Soviet Union, with each controlling different zones. Until the signing of the treaty, the question of Austria's future geopolitical alignment was a source of early Cold War tensions, and the country became a potential hot spot. The treaty entailed the occupying powers' recognizing Austrian independence and its territorial integrity and withdrawing their forces from its territory.[8] In a linked step, the Austrian parliament established the country's permanent neutrality through a constitutional amendment. This arrangement removed Austria as a Cold War battleground and paved the way for a long period of prosperity in the country. Neutrality even fostered a distinctive Austrian national identity.[9]

The largest in-between state, Ukraine, has a complicated history with MSGs. In the 1994 Budapest Memorandum, the United States, the United Kingdom, and Russia promised to respect Ukraine's sovereignty and territorial integrity in exchange for that country's pledge to relinquish its nuclear weapons and accede to the Nuclear Non-Proliferation Treaty.[10] According to Oleksandr Chalyi, one of the Ukrainian diplomats who negotiated the document, there was an implicit assumption of nonalignment in the Budapest Memorandum:

> The Budapest Memorandum was, in essence, a particular form of international recognition of the status of Ukraine as a neutral state, because it implies that for issues related to its national security, Ukraine must not take the side of one of its guarantors against the interests of another. . . . After signing the Budapest Memorandum, Ukraine could have further strengthened its status as a permanently neutral state by both following the principles of neutrality in its foreign policy de facto and by seeking

---

8 Austria, France, Soviet Union, United Kingdom, and United States, Treaty for the Re-Establishment of an Independent and Democratic Austria, Vienna, May 15, 1955.

9 Johanna Rainio-Niemi, "Cold War Neutrality in Europe: Lessons to Be Learned?" in Heinz Gartner, ed., *Engaged Neutrality: An Evolved Approach to the Cold War*, Lanham, Md.: Lexington Books, 2017, p. 27.

10 United Nations (UN), Letter Dated 7 December 1994 from the Permanent Representatives of the Russian Federation, Ukraine, the United Kingdom of Great Britain and Northern Ireland and the United States of America to the United Nations Addressed to the Secretary-General, December 19, 1994.

> international legal recognition of its neutral status by other states and international organizations. Unfortunately, history did not unfold this way.[11]

The failure of the Budapest Memorandum vividly illustrates the limits of such documents, particularly when implicit assumptions are made about the conditions of the arrangement.

Proposed MSGs

Unlike Budapest, the MSGs we propose would be explicit about the conditions under which the guarantees are valid, because there would be a clear reciprocal bargain: The in-between state in question would embrace nonaligned status and fulfill its obligations under that status in return for guarantees from the major powers that they would respect its sovereignty and security. Additionally, the MSGs we propose would have an exit clause that would allow the guarantors or the guaranteed parties to leave the arrangement if the other side violates its end of the bargain. If one side does not uphold its side of the bargain, then the other side does not have to abide by its end. Additionally, these guarantees could be codified in a legally binding UN Security Council resolution, whereas the Budapest Memorandum was a politically binding document. Finally, our proposed MSGs are supplemented by CSBMs (see next section) that demonstrate commitment and provide early warning of any potential violation of the conditions of the guarantee.

It should be noted that, while this approach offers a corrective to the shortcomings of the Budapest Memorandum, no agreement could prevent a powerful state that is determined to violate its terms from doing so. Agreements such as the one we propose establish norms and standards of behavior by which states' behavior is judged. These agreements thus raise the reputational costs of noncompliance and create incentives to stick to the terms. But the belief of the parties that observing an agreement is in their interests is the best guarantee of compliance. Because the MSGs we propose would be endorsed by the major

[11] Oleksandr Chalyi, "Approaches to Resolving the Conflict over the States In Between," in Charap, Demus, and Shapiro, 2018, pp. 34–35.

powers and would be consistent with their respective interests, our proposal would eliminate incentives to violate the guarantees.

The guarantees would not resolve specific existing conflicts in the region. But this revision of the security architecture would provide a strong impetus to conflict settlement or, at least, more-effective conflict management; Chapter Four describes mechanisms to achieve these objectives. Conflict settlement has important linkages to MSGs; an in-between state will be unlikely to accept security assurances from a power it considers to be violating its territorial integrity. Conversely, progress toward agreement on a revised security architecture is necessary to create a geopolitical context in which those disputes can be more effectively addressed.

In addition to traditional security, the MSGs should also provide explicit reassurance that there will not be inappropriate external interference by major powers in the internal affairs of the states that adopt the third way. This would cover so-called *gray zone* activities—that is, instruments and actions below the threshold of military intervention, including the use of cyberspace for coercive purposes.

CSBMs

CSBMs are intended to demonstrate commitment to the MSGs, define what it means to adhere to those MSGs on the ground, and provide early warning of potential violations. Such measures could include military restraint and transparency measures and cooperative security instruments that address disputes and deescalate potential crises. To be effective, such measures must address the security concerns and threat perceptions of the parties. The measures described below represent a menu of possible options that could be adapted for particular contexts. (See Table 2.1 for a summary.) Many of the proposals have been adapted from existing CSBM and conventional arms control regimes—such as the Vienna Document,[12] a politically binding agreement that requires the exchange and verification of information about armed forces and military activities—for the specific security

[12] OSCE, Vienna Document 2011: On Confidence- and Security-Building Measures, Vienna, November 30, 2011.

Table 2.1
Summary of Proposed CSBMs to Complement the MSGs

Guarantor Powers	Members of Alliances Bordering Third-Way States	States That Adopt the Third Way
• No stationing of forces on the territory of in-between states that adopt the third way • No covert intelligence-gathering or other hostile activities aimed against other signatories of the arrangement on the territory of in-between states that adopt the third way • Mutually agreed and scheduled withdrawal of forces currently deployed on the territory of the third-way states • Compliance with limits on temporary deployments in third-way states	• Limitation on deployments and exercises in a defined zone of the member bordering an in-between state that adopts the third way • Ban on snap exercises in the zone • Information exchange on deployments within the border zone • Regular verification of that information • Prior notification of military activities in the zone • Observation of specified military activities within the zone • Third-party verification within the zone	• No permanent stationing of foreign combat forces or use of military infrastructure by foreign nations • No use of their territory for other states' covert intelligence-gathering or other hostile activities • Limits on size of temporary deployments of foreign forces • Notification of temporary deployments of foreign forces

challenges addressed in this volume. The obligations would differ for the guarantor powers offering the MSGs, member states of military alliances bordering in-between states that adopt the third way, and the third-way states themselves.

Military restraint measures can provide countries that adopt the third way with reassurance that the risk of a surprise attack across their borders is minimal. To this effect, the parties should agree on a comprehensive set of specific constraints and transparency measures, which would apply in defined zones of member states of military alliances bordering those nonaligned states that adopt the third way. Such measures would address threat perceptions regarding the possibility of a rapid concentration of forces in the vicinity of the borders of nonaligned countries.[13] Restraint measures would cover ground forces permanently stationed within the defined zone that are capable of carrying out combined arms cross-border operations on short notice; the size, frequency, and duration of temporary deployments within the zone; and the size, frequency, and duration of military activities (e.g., exercises) in the defined zone.

For example, temporary deployments from outside the zone, out-of-garrison activities of ground forces permanently stationed within the area, or both could be limited to the level of one division. There would be no more than two military exercises per year involving one brigade or more in the zone, and the duration of such exercises would be limited to no more than two weeks. The total number of troops involved in parallel exercises would not exceed the established limit for temporary deployments and exercises (in this case, one division).

---

[13] Specific measures suggested in this section are largely inspired by discussions within the project *Reducing the Risks of Conventional Deterrence in Europe: Arms Control in the NATO-Russia Contact Zones*, implemented by the OSCE Network of Think Tanks and Academic Institutions and, particularly, by the contribution of Wolfgang Richter to the Moscow workshop on November 7, 2018. See Wolfgang Zellner, Philip Remler, Wolfgang Richter, Andrei Zagorski, Evgeny P. Buzhinsky, Vladislav L. Chernov, Ali Serdar Erdurmaz, Marc Finaud, Cornelius Friesendorf, P. Terrence Hopmann, Lukasz Kelsa, Igors Rajevs, Benjamin Schaller, Hans-Joachim Schmidt, Niklas Schörnig, Oleg Shakirov, and Simon Weiß, *Reducing the Risks of Conventional Deterrence in Europe: Arms Control in the NATO-Russia Contact Zones*, Vienna: OSCE Network of Think Tanks and Academic Institutions, 2018.

Unannounced snap exercises would not be allowed in the specified border zone.

A set of transparency and verification measures that go beyond existing CSBMs and are specific to these defined zones should be agreed to increase predictability, avoid surprises, and reduce uncertainty. Such measures could include the following:

- information exchange on ground forces permanently stationed within the border zone and available reinforcement infrastructure, including prepositioned equipment in storage facilities
- regular verification (on-site inspections) of the information provided
- prior notification of military activities (temporary deployment from outside the zone and out-of-garrison activities above a specified level)
- observation of specified military activities (e.g., exercises) within the zone
- the possibility of third-party verification (e.g., through the OSCE) at the request of any party.

In return for these restraint and transparency commitments from the major powers and their allies, the third-way countries would pledge not to allow any permanent stationing of foreign combat forces or use of military infrastructure on their territory by foreign nations. They would also pledge not to allow any use of their territory for covert intelligence-gathering or other hostile activities aimed at any of the countries that have provided them with security guarantees. Any temporary deployments of foreign troops on the territory of nonaligned countries (e.g., for the purposes of exercises) would be subject to transparency measures and could also be limited to a certain level.

The guarantor powers would commit not to station combat forces on the territory of the states that adopt the third way and not to use those states' territory for covert intelligence-gathering or other hostile activities aimed against other guarantors. This commitment would entail a mutually agreed and scheduled withdrawal of those forces of the guarantor powers that are currently deployed on the territory of the nonaligned third-way states. The guarantors would also commit to complying with the measures that apply to temporary foreign troop deployments on the territory of nonaligned states that adopt the third way.

Multilateral consultative mechanisms should be established allowing the parties to these arrangements to address any concerns regarding compliance with these commitments. Such mechanisms would encompass regular meetings (i.e., conferences of the parties) to review the implementation of the arrangement, and extraordinary meetings to address particular issues of concern. Measures to prevent unintended escalation of any dangerous military incidents could also be established, such as hotlines between relevant operational headquarters, continuous exchange of information on and explanation of military activities, a significant increase of military-to-military contacts, and the establishment of permanent military liaison teams.

These CSBMs are, in a sense, the mechanisms for implementing the commitments contained in the third-way status and the MSGs. The in-between states that adopt the third way cease allowing activities on their territory—such as permanent deployments—that one or more guarantors might consider indicative of de facto alignment or alliance. The guarantors cease conducting such activities on third-way states' territory and withdraw forces currently deployed there to demonstrate their commitment to the nonalignment and security of the third-way states. By accepting limits on their military activities along the border of the third-way states, the guarantors further reassure the latter that they will not be postured for aggression. Such measures will also increase warning and decisionmaking time, which is critical in times of crisis.

Enhanced Security for All

Together, these pieces—RSCs, associated norms of behavior, a third-way status offer for nonaligned countries, and a package of MSGs and CSBMs intended to reassure those accepting the third-way status—would constitute a major upgrade of the security architecture. This proposed revision of the regional security architecture at its core works by seeking major-power buy-in to the status of in-between states, reassuring all parties that changes to the status quo will only occur through a mechanism of regional consultation in which they have a presence, and providing instruments to create on-the-ground confidence that the system is working. The major powers will therefore have much less incentive to destabilize the in-between states in the hope of achieving some advantage over their rivals. All parties would be more secure and the region would be subject to less destructive conflict.

Those in-between states that choose to adopt the third way would exchange their ambitions to join alliances—that remain unfulfilled while nonetheless causing instability and thus creating insecurity—with a more realistic offer that provides immediate security benefits. These benefits include major-power endorsement of their status, MSGs, and concrete mechanisms to create confidence that they can maintain their nonaligned status without interference and threats to their security. In return, those states would commit to consult with the permanent participants of the RSC on future changes in their status. They would also significantly increase the chances of resolving their territorial disputes through the mechanisms described in Chapter Four.

Critically, the revised order also tries to allow for a degree of flexibility so that future changes in the preferences of in-between states can be accommodated in a manner that would not threaten the overall system and would not lead to armed conflict or great-power tensions. As we saw in Ukraine in 2013 and 2014, dramatic shifts in foreign policy preferences can be highly destabilizing. The proposed system would address this problem through both the consultation mechanism and the norm that requires consultations and attempts to find consensus on changes in the regional security architecture. Currently aligned states that, for whatever reason, want to leave their alliance could adopt the third way status without risk of retribution from any of the major powers. Countries would only be able to shift from membership in one bloc to membership in the other after consultations and attempts to find consensus. Thus, even a domestic revolution that dramatically changes a given state's foreign policy preferences would not lead to sudden, unilateral shifts in alignment.

Compliance with the provisions outlined here will be a concern for all parties involved. Today, mutual mistrust is rampant, particularly between Russia and the West (and several of Russia's neighbors). This mistrust causes both sides to believe that the other will abuse any agreement for unilateral gain. Our proposal provides for compliance through the mutual bargain that is the core of the third-way offer: an in-between state's commitment to nonalignment in return for major powers' commitment to that state's security. If one party violates its side of the bargain, the other is no longer bound by its commitments. Beyond that, the norms we propose would raise the reputational costs of noncompliance and therefore incentivize sticking to the agreement. "But," as an earlier publication of this project notes, "the best guarantee of compliance is an accord that all key players believe to be in their interests."[14] Fundamentally, the effectiveness of the revised architecture we propose rests on the core interests of the parties. Such a foundation is likely to provide for far more durable compliance than any enforcement provision.

Proof of Concept: A Belarus Scenario

The impact of the proposal is perhaps best illustrated by a hypothetical situation involving a currently allied state that seeks to exit its alliance. We have chosen Belarus for this purpose, but the principles are equally applicable to a NATO member state that desires to leave its alliance. The scenario is meant to show how the revised architecture would be resilient to political changes.

Belarus is a Russian ally and the only in-between state with no territorial conflicts. It has a two-decade-long history of poor relations with the West, and is only now slowly improving relations with the EU and the United States. At the same time, Minsk has been the most active participant in Russian-driven integration projects since the mid-1990s. It is a member of the CSTO and, therefore, aligned with Moscow. Since 1999, it has been in a Union State with Russia, and hosts two Russian military facilities on its territory.

[14] Charap, Shapiro, and Demus, 2018, p. 22.

The huge asymmetry in Minsk's relations with Russia and the West is a problem for Belarusian security, because it makes Belarus too dependent on Russia and thus too vulnerable to the latter's pressure. Accordingly, Belarusian foreign policy seeks to ensure some freedom of maneuver and balance between Russia and the West (and other major powers when relevant), despite its alliance with Moscow. Minsk seeks some independence from Moscow, while profiting from economic openness toward the West and avoiding becoming a battleground in a major-power confrontation.[15]

These imperatives lead to a type of foreign policy behavior known in international relations theory as *hedging*, which is about spreading risk and broadening foreign and security policy options and space for maneuvering.[16] Thus, Belarus makes a strategic effort not only to stay out of the major powers' confrontation but also to offer itself as a bridge-builder between them.[17] As a result, there is a structurally driven salience of nonalignment ideas and inclinations in Belarusian foreign policy. The point of this flirtation with nonalignment is not to abandon the alliance with Russia; nonetheless, it does pose challenges for Minsk's relations with Moscow.

A shift in Belarusian foreign policy, while certainly unlikely at this point in time, could result from a sudden change in either the domestic political or international contexts. Such a shift could reinforce the country's inclinations toward nonalignment. New leadership in Minsk might in theory even seek to leave the CSTO. If recent experience is any guide, under the current security architecture, the West would celebrate such a development as an opportunity to deepen ties with Belarus, while Russia would see it as a threat—not only to its role in the region, but to its own domestic stability and national security.

---

[15] Yauheni Preiherman, "Belarus Finds Its Foreign Policy Stride," *Global Brief*, Fall/Winter 2019.

[16] Kendall W. Stiles, *Trust and Hedging in International Relations*, Ann Arbor, Mich.: University of Michigan Press, 2018.

[17] "Lukashenko: Idea to Launch New International Negotiating Process Gains More Supporters," BelTA, October 31, 2018.

It is not hard to imagine Russia taking forceful action to prevent such an outcome.

But it is also clear that Russia would incur significant costs if it were to do so. As in Ukraine, a Russian conflict with Belarus would destroy its popularity in the country, sow permanent instability on its border, and likely saddle it with yet another economic basket case which it would need to subsidize heavily. It would result in further rounds of Western sanctions, and probably increase NATO force posture on the Russian border. None of this would ultimately be very popular in Russia itself; however, the prospect of Belarus exiting the alliance and potentially seeking NATO membership would leave Moscow with no other choice but to act.

In the proposed revised architecture, Russia would have another choice. Under the system we propose, a fundamental reorientation of Belarus's alignment (in this case, in favor of NATO membership) without a consultative process is not possible. Instead, if Belarus were to decide to leave the CSTO, the RSC would convene, and Minsk could request third-way nonaligned status, along with a tailored package of MSGs and CSBMs. These measures would provide for Belarusian security and also guarantee that despite Minsk's exit from its alliance with Russia, it would not be joining the Western camp. Instead, its security and nonalignment would be guaranteed by all major powers. Of course, even this would not be easy for Russia to accept, but it would be far more palatable than the alternative.

The revised architecture would therefore be able to adapt to changes in an in-between state's foreign policy through a mechanism of major-power consultation that prevents those changes from becoming a *casus belli*.

Conclusion

Of course, if the goal of either Russia or the West is to pursue nothing less than total hegemony over the in-between states, this new system will not work. In that case, one side will violate the agreements and we could return to the status quo.

But this proposed architecture at least tests the proposition that mutually acceptable compromise could be possible, rather than simply assuming the tragedy of great-power competition will always prevail and taking steps to make that a reality. A failure of this proposal will not worsen the situation relative to today. By contrast, continuing with the status quo will practically ensure that all such developments in Belarus (or other in-between states) will result in increased instability and possibly civil or even major-power war. Avoiding that outcome seems worth the effort.

CHAPTER THREE

Economic Integration

Alexandra Dienes, Sergey Afontsev, Péter Balás, Rodica Crudu, Diana Galoyan

For the in-between states, improved trade relations with neighbors, including the European Union (EU) and Eurasian Economic Union (EAEU) blocs, are vital for economic growth and prosperity. However, the mutual incompatibility of the integration agendas of the two blocs—along with the political and military tensions in the region—has led to the disruption of economic connectivity. As integration initiatives have increasingly become mutually incompatible, the costs for the in-between states of choosing between them has skyrocketed; at its most extreme, the *either/or* trap has led to military conflict. Even Azerbaijan, which has managed to stay out of the clash of competing regional integration projects, has lost economic opportunities from the negative side effects of the disputes between Moscow and Brussels.

The in-between states need not bear the ever-increasing costs associated with their geographical position. Besides contributing to economic progress in in-between states themselves, efforts that cooperatively address economic integration could bring European and Russian stakeholders closer together, thus promoting mutual trust and a sense of common interest. Just as preparations for a conflict can start a vicious cycle of conflict escalation, negotiating strategies of cooperation can reduce mistrust and promote wider partnership.

While substantial effort has been put into identifying who is to blame for the current tensions, the only result has been conflicting narratives about the origins of the conflict. The economic costs of the impasse have led to the accumulation of losses for all sides and have blocked opportunities to move toward the longer-term goals of continent-wide economic integration. Meanwhile, issues that would have been previously considered technical in nature—and thus best left to seasoned negotiators to find agreement—have now become sparks for further political conflict. So far, relevant governments have generated few forward-looking solutions, even though all parties agree on the undesirability of the current situation.

Envisioning a parallel negotiation to the other two tracks identified in this volume, this chapter looks over the horizon and lays out a proposal for developing a more cooperative approach to relations among the EU, the in-between states, and Russia and the EAEU. It would be difficult to make significant progress on the economic track without addressing the regional conflicts and the security architecture. These disputes have created too much political friction to allow technical trade talks to succeed. Therefore, our proposal assumes parallel progress on talks regarding regional conflicts and the security architecture. It would not be possible to implement the changes we suggest without progress in those parallel discussions. We further assume that all parties will make good-faith efforts to address each other's existing concerns about compliance with World Trade Organization (WTO) norms and other international commitments. Such efforts will be necessary in order for all parties to have the confidence to enter into any new agreements.

Our proposal consists of three parts: measures to facilitate multidirectional trade relations for in-between states; trilateral consultation mechanisms among the EAEU, the EU, and nonmembers of the two blocs; and agreed norms of behavior for the blocs.

Caught In-Between: Threats and Opportunities

On its face, being in between two major trading blocs is neither a blessing nor a curse. Figure 3.1 uses a strengths, weaknesses, opportunities, and threats (SWOT) analysis to demonstrate both the internal strengths and weaknesses and the external opportunities and threats inherent in this position. It shows that the most significant weakness is the limited agency of the respective countries, as bargaining positions

Figure 3.1
A SWOT Analysis of the Economic Aspects of In-Between Status

Strengths	Weaknesses
• Neighbors depend on transit through in-between states' territory for trade	• Limited agency with larger, neighboring powers
Opportunities	**Threats**
• Trade and investment diversification • Balancing conflicting interests of neighboring powers to benefit from both sides	• Excessive economic reliance on one of the partners (e.g., over- and under-trading with particular neighboring countries) • Either/or choice in economic integration

are, in most cases, dominated by neighboring powers. However, this weakness can be neutralized by taking advantage of opportunities to balance against the conflicting interests of larger neighboring powers. The states between the EU and EAEU have the inherent ability to maneuver between them.

Meanwhile, close relations stemming from historical legacies, economic agreements, or both can result in excessive economic reliance on one partner, while the cooperation opportunities with other partners remain limited. This threat can be further aggravated if the neighboring powers propose conflicting economic agreements or integration projects, and expect the in-between countries to make a choice between them. In this case, being forced to choose between mutually exclusive integration initiatives can result in economic hardships and political tensions, which sometimes lead to conflicts with serious security challenges and high economic costs.

Economically, the most promising opportunity arises from trade and investment diversification: a win-win strategy that allows the in-between state to thrive along with all neighbors. Additionally, in-between states can use economic diplomacy strategies to take advantage of the potentially conflicting interests of the neighboring powers and their competition for the political and economic loyalty of those states.

The Status Quo

The six in-between states fall into three categories: (1) signatories of a Deep and Comprehensive Free Trade Area (DCFTA) agreement with the EU (Georgia, Moldova, and Ukraine); (2) EAEU members (Armenia and Belarus); and (3) Azerbaijan, which has not sought integration with either bloc. It is important to note that the DCFTA is much more than a free trade agreement: The state signatories commit to harmonize key elements of domestic legislation with the *acquis communautaire*—the EU's laws and rules. The EAEU grew out of the Eurasian Customs Union, which was founded in 2009 by Russia, Belarus, and Kazakhstan (Armenia and Kyrgyzstan joined in 2015). In addition to a unified external tariff and customs border, the EAEU seeks to open financial and labor markets to allow for the free flow of goods and people across the bloc.[1] Meanwhile, Armenia, Belarus, Moldova, and Ukraine (along with Russia) signed on to the Commonwealth of Independent States (CIS) free trade area agreement (FTA) in 2011, which, among other provisions, reinstated and further elaborated principles of duty-free movement of goods and nondiscrimination of producers.[2]

The downturn in relations between the EU and Russia, coupled with a series of mutual trade restrictions, has affected their bilateral economic relationship and EU trade relations with other EAEU members. In the past, policymakers on both sides had envisioned a common economic space stretching from Lisbon, Portugal, on the EU's Atlantic flank, to Russia's Pacific city of Vladivostok.[3] Instead, the two

---

[1] International Institute for Strategic Studies, "Eurasia's Economic Bloc at Risk from Geopolitics," *Strategic Comments*, Vol. 21, No. 5, October 2015, pp. xi–xii.

[2] Commonwealth of Independent States, Treaty on a Free-Trade Area, St. Petersburg, Russia, October 18, 2011.

[3] See, for example, the reference to the "common humanitarian and economic space from the Atlantic to the Pacific" in the declaration issued by the leaders of Russia, Germany, France, and Ukraine simultaneously with the signing of the so-called Minsk II agreement

integration initiatives—which, if made compatible, could have presented opportunities for dynamic economic growth for the in-between states—are mutually exclusive efforts, turning regional economic integration into a zero-sum game. Moreover, issues such as phytosanitary standards (which previously would have been left to technocrats to negotiate) now regularly risk sparking political disputes. An apt example would be the current turbulence in Russia-Moldova trade.

Currently, both the EU and Russia suspect the other is trying to "poach" away its in-between partners and bring them to the other side. The EU and EAEU have no official dialogue, let alone formal agreements.[4] Brussels instituted a policy of not engaging with the EAEU in 2014, which has been interpreted in Moscow as an indication that the EU does not respect the legitimacy of the EAEU, thus implicitly seeking to undermine it.[5] Similarly, many in EU capitals believe Moscow seeks to weaken and undermine the EU.[6]

The Paths of the Six In-Between States

The economic integration experiences of the six in-between countries are diverse (see Figures 3.2 and 3.3). After initial friction, Armenia has partially been able to overcome the either/or trap and build relations with both of its important partners. In late 2013, Armenia was on the cusp of signing a DCFTA with the EU, but abruptly changed course and decided to join the Eurasian Customs Union and, thus, the

---

in February 2015 (President of Russia, "Deklaratsiya Prezidenta Rossiiskoi Federatsii, Prezidenta Ukrainy, Prezidenta Frantsuzskoi Respubliki i Kantslera Federativnoi Respubliki Germaniya v podderzhku Kompleksa mer po vypolneniyu Minskikh soglashenii," February 12, 2015).

4 As of June 2019, technical working-level talks between the European Commission and the Eurasian Economic Commission (the executive bodies of the two blocs) have restarted.

5 As one Russian observer put it, "Brussels still doesn't acknowledge the existence of the EAEU, or more specifically its international legal standing, and 'doubts its supranational character,' and therefore officially rules out formal cooperation." Yuri Kofner, "Desyat' prichin, pochemu EAES i ES stoit sotrudnichat'," Valdai Club, June 26, 2019. The EU maintains that it has cut off formal contacts because of Russian actions toward Ukraine since 2014.

6 See, for example, Michał Broniatowski, "Tusk Makes Scathing Attack on Russian Influence," *Politico Europe,* October 6, 2018.

Figure 3.2
In-Between States' Exports to Russia and the EU as a Percentage of Total Exports, 2010 Versus 2018

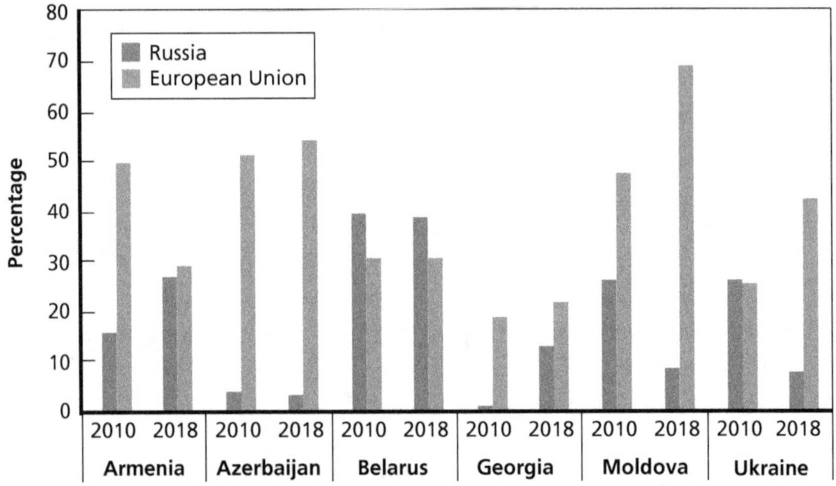

SOURCE: UN Comtrade data, accessed August 20, 2019.

EAEU. As a result, changes in Armenia's export structure are especially remarkable: Between 2010 and 2018, the percentage of total exports to Russia increased by 11.1 percent, while the percentage of total exports to the EU decreased by 20.9 percent.

Despite its EAEU membership, Armenia found a way to strengthen relations with the EU, signing a Comprehensive and Enhanced Partnership Agreement (CEPA) in 2017.[7] The CEPA is comprehensive, addressing both economic ties and political issues. It also covers legal cooperation, the rule of law, combating money laundering and terrorist financing, and fighting organized crime and corruption. The agreement establishes a solid legal basis for strengthening political dialogue, broadening the scope of economic and sectoral cooperation, creating a framework for new opportunities in trade and investments,

---

[7] European Union External Action Service, "New Agreement Signed Between the European Union and Armenia Set to Bring Tangible Benefits to Citizens," Brussels, November 24, 2017.

Figure 3.3
In-Between States' Imports from Russia and the EU as a Percentage of Total Imports, 2010 Versus 2018

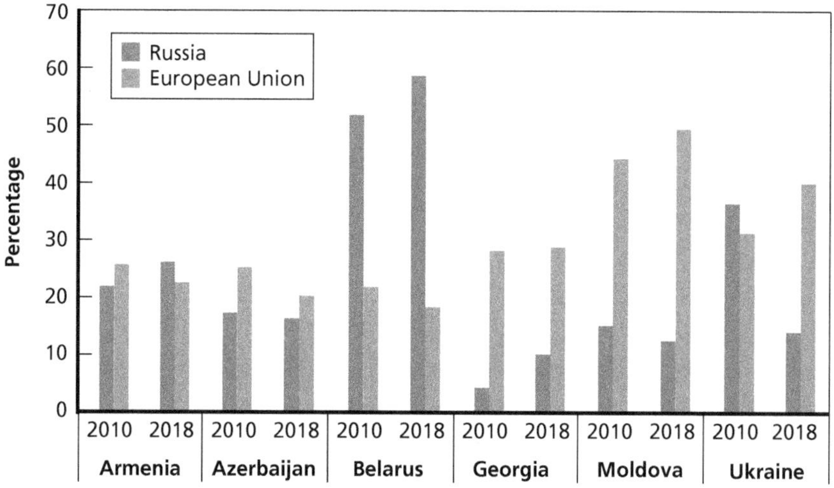

SOURCE: UN Comtrade data, accessed August 10, 2019.

and increasing mobility for citizens. In certain areas, the CEPA is also designed to gradually harmonize some elements of Armenian law with the EU *acquis*. It does not, however, go so far as to establish a free trade zone between the EU and Armenia or touch any EAEU competencies. Given the circumstances of its EAEU membership, Armenia found perhaps the most balance possible in its external economic relations through the CEPA with the EU.

Azerbaijan has joined neither the EU nor EAEU, instead seeking cooperation with both blocs. Both partners' shares of trade with Baku have remained stable from 2010 through 2018. This can be explained, at least in part, by the structure of Azerbaijan's exports, which largely consist of oil and gas.

Though a founding member of the EAEU, Belarus's membership has not prevented it from developing economic relations with the EU, which represents 18 percent of its imports and 30 percent of its exports. A continuing issue preventing formal engagement between the EU and

Minsk is that Belarus has not yet joined the WTO, as discussed in greater detail in a later section.[8]

Georgia's experience has been somewhat like that of Armenia. In the early 2000s, Georgia and Russia had friendly relations, and Russia accounted for 16 percent of Georgia's total trade.[9] Relations soured in the run-up to the 2008 Russia-Georgia conflict: Starting in 2006, Russia imposed a series of trade embargoes on Georgian exports.[10] Mutual trade collapsed as a result, with Russia's share of Georgia's external trade plummeting to just 4 percent in 2010.[11] However, Russia agreed in 2009 to apply the CIS FTA to Georgian exports—despite Georgia's withdrawal from the CIS—and in 2012 Georgia began a cautious and gradual normalization of economic relations with Russia. Simultaneously, Tbilisi was pursuing a DCFTA, which it eventually signed in 2014, and began implementing reforms aimed at liberalizing foreign trade and customs procedures, imposing low import tariffs, and simplifying tariff and nontariff rules, which have contributed to the economy's resilience to external shocks and reduced the vulnerability of its current account.[12] Although Moscow threatened to retaliate after Tbilisi signed the DCFTA, it did not follow through on the threat.[13] Consequently, Georgia became the only country in the region that has both a DCFTA with the EU and functioning trade with Russia. Notably, the application of the CIS FTA to trade between Georgia and Russia is important not only for Tbilisi but also for Yere-

---

8 Ewa Synoweic, "The EU Is Encouraging Belarus to Join the World Trade Organisation," *Emerging Europe*, December 30, 2016.

9 UN Comtrade data as of August 10, 2019.

10 C. J. Chivers, "A Russian 'Wine Blockade' Against Georgia and Moldova," *New York Times*, April 6, 2006.

11 UN Comtrade data, accessed August 10, 2019.

12 Amat Adarov and Peter Havlik, *Benefits and Costs of DCFTA: Evaluation of the Impact on Georgia, Moldova, and Ukraine*, joint working paper, Vienna: Vienna Institute for International Economic Studies and Bertelsmann Stiftung, December 2016.

13 Denis Cenusa, Michael Emerson, Tamara Kovziridse, and Veronika Movchan, *Russia's Punitive Trade Policy Measures Towards Ukraine, Moldova and Georgia*, Brussels: Centre for European Policy Studies, CEPS Working Document, No. 400, September 2014, pp. 7–8.

van, since transit through Georgia is Armenia's only linkage with other EAEU member states.

Moldova's EU DCFTA also came into effect in 2016, and has helped drive the country's shift in trade increasingly toward the EU and away from Russia. Between 2010 and 2018, the share of Moldovan exports to the EU increased by 21.5 percent, while the percentage of exports to Russia dropped by 18.1 percent. Moldovan imports showed more-moderate changes (5.2 and –2.7 percent, respectively). In addition to its geographical reorientation, Moldova has registered structural changes in its exported commodity range, mainly because of the higher standards required by the EU market, especially in the field of machinery and transport equipment.

During and after Moldova's DCFTA negotiation process, Russia implemented several commercial restrictions, alleging insufficient quality standards. These targeted alcoholic beverages (2013); processed meat (2014); and wine, fruits, and canned vegetables (2014).[14] Eventually, tariffs were raised on these imports in a formal government decree.[15] Although Russian restrictions had a negative impact on individual sectors, they did not cause serious problems for the Moldovan economy more broadly because Moldova's trade structure had already begun to reorient toward the EU market.

Moscow's decision to apply customs tariffs remains in force, though both sides have agreed to suspend it. The parties agreed to suspend the Russian customs duties for certain Moldovan products from January 1, 2019, to June 30, 2019.[16] But this agreement was almost immediately eclipsed by another event: In the context of its ongoing trade war with Ukraine, Russia blocked imports transiting through Ukrainian territory (including those of Moldovan origin). However, Chisinau almost immediately managed to find a compromise with

---

[14] Kamil Całus, "Russian Sanctions Against Moldova: Minor Effects, Major Potential," Centre for Eastern Studies, November 6, 2014.

[15] Government of the Russian Federation, On the Introduction of Imported Customs Duties for Goods from the Republic of Moldova, Resolution No. 736, July 31, 2014 (as amended on December 30, 2018).

[16] Government of the Russian Federation, 2014.

Moscow that allowed for transit through Ukraine to resume.[17] These developments seemed to be highly politicized.

Until 2014, Ukraine's trade with Russia and the EU was approximately equal. However, Russia suspended the CIS FTA regime toward Ukraine in 2016, after the EU-Ukraine DCFTA entered into force, arguing that Ukraine's participation in both would pose risks for Russia's own economy.[18] In addition to this move, which drastically increased tariffs on Ukrainian goods, Moscow also banned agricultural imports from Ukraine; in turn, Kyiv banned a range of Russian imports, ranging from meat to alcohol products.[19] As a result of these mutual sanctions and the broader conflict, trade with Russia collapsed (exports dropped by almost 340 percent and imports by 260 percent). By 2018, Ukraine's trade turnover with the EU was almost four times greater than its trade with Russia.[20] Such a drop appears to overshoot the potential equilibrium in bilateral trade based on economic fundamentals, much in the same way as the drop in trade between Russia and Georgia after 2008, with chances for correction when (and if) bilateral relations see a thaw. If the conditions of the CIS FTA remain suspended, it will be much harder for Ukraine to restore its trade with Russia. Moldova would suffer as well, as its ability to transit goods via Ukraine will continually be disrupted.

It is important to note that this chapter does not address the broader political elements of EU integration beyond the DCFTAs that Moldova, Georgia, and Ukraine have undertaken. Indeed, the DCFTAs are merely one component of EU Association Agreements that the three signed. These documents address a range of issues, from collaboration with the EU on foreign policy to criminal justice reform.

---

[17] "Dodon soobshchil, chto dogovorilsya s Putinym o tranzite moldavskikh tovarov cherez Ukrainu," TASS, January 30, 2019.

[18] "Russia Suspends Free Trade Agreement with Ukraine," *Moscow Times*, December 16, 2015.

[19] Samuel Charap and Timothy J. Colton, *Everyone Loses: The Ukraine Crisis and the Ruinous Contest for Post-Soviet Eurasia*, Abingdon, UK: Routledge, 2017, pp. 148–150.

[20] UN Comtrade data as of August 10, 2019.

Proposal

Ideally, the vision of Lisbon to Vladivostok—i.e., a common economic space spanning the EU, the EAEU, and the in-between states—could be realized. But today's reality is so far removed from that vision that it can be considered only as a long-term objective. Instead of focusing on such grand designs, we propose to adjust and build on current economic arrangements to reduce frictions and increase prosperity for all.

It is important to begin with an understanding of which arrangements are and are not possible for the in-between states. An in-between state cannot be a member of both the EU and EAEU, since both blocs are customs unions. Since customs unions negotiate trade agreements collectively, EAEU members cannot sign bilateral DCFTAs with the EU. DCFTA signatories have made commitments (to implement a range of EU standards and adjust their tariffs) that make EAEU membership impossible. It is, however, possible for an in-between state to be party to multiple FTAs (including a DCFTA). More broadly, it is possible for nonmembers to establish enhanced economic relations with both blocs. And it is possible for the blocs themselves to agree on mutually acceptable arrangements.

As an alternative to the status quo, whereby incompatibilities cause frictions, we propose a way forward for the in-between states that builds on options that can be combined. Our proposal provides an opportunity for in-between states to benefit from trading with both blocs, rather than fully siding with one of them and losing out on connectivity with the other.[21] Such a development would help in-between states become more prosperous and stable. It would also help them develop agency with both the EU and Russia and the EAEU, rather than opportunistically showing loyalty to one or the other side and receiving economic benefits as a reward. The goals of the proposal are the following:

[21] All parties making good faith efforts to address each other's existing concerns about compliance with WTO and other international commitments will be necessary in order for them to have the confidence necessary to enter into new agreements.

- ensure that economic relations are not a source of conflict, either between Russia and the EU or between Russia and in-between states
- facilitate in-between states' prosperity through enhanced economic ties, thus providing incentives for these states to engage on the other two negotiation tracks: security architecture and regional conflicts.

Our proposal consists of the following three elements:

1. measures to facilitate multidirectional trade relations for in-between states
2. trilateral consultation mechanisms among the EAEU, the EU, and nonmembers of the two blocs
3. agreed norms of behavior for the blocs.

Multidirectional Trade Relations

Multidirectional trade relations, by which we mean establishment of a functioning and mutually beneficial trade regime for in-between states with both the EU and EAEU, can facilitate economic diversification. By spreading risk and making in-between states less reliant on single trade partners, such relations can make the interdependent relationships in the region healthier. Economic diversification includes broadening the geographic spread of one's trade partners and increasing the range of goods that are traded with external partners. Although the economic effects of such diversification are likely to differ based on the country's development status and position in global value chains, the political effects would be similar for all in-between states: It would increase these states' agency and provide them with leverage to escape the either/or trap.

We propose several EU-EAEU arrangements and specific formulas for each of the in-between states to achieve the goals of multidirectional trade relations. DCFTA signatories need mutually beneficial frameworks for trading relations with Russia and the EAEU. The in-between states that are EAEU members need arrangements that facilitate their economic engagement with the EU. And Azerbaijan, which remains fully outside the blocs, could benefit from a framework for enhanced ties with both.

Measures to Improve EU-EAEU Ties

Achieving multidirectional trade relations for any of the in-between states would be facilitated by EU-EAEU arrangements, as the current lack of formal cooperation contributes to the zero-sum dynamic. Although the EU refuses to engage with the EAEU as a bloc, one could imagine that policy changing if the other two elements of the regional order were to be addressed in parallel. (Belarus would also need to become a member of the WTO because the EU requires all EAEU participants to join the WTO before it can make additional arrangements with the bloc.) Three EU-EAEU arrangements would be desirable under those circumstances.

First, the parties could establish a permanent EU-EAEU task force to harmonize technical regulations and deconflict transit issues, paying special attention to the interests of in-between states and the legal obligations they have toward both regional blocs. The ability of in-between states to improve their trade relations with the two blocs is contingent primarily on mechanisms preventing contradictions between obligations for EAEU members and EU norms. Many technical standards between the EU and the EAEU are compatible already. Over the years, the EAEU has sought to approximate its standards to the EU or international technical standards and regulations. In cases where standards are incompatible, mutual recognition of standards is an option. Regulatory convergence would mean that in-between states would have significantly reduced transaction costs.

Second, a framework agreement between the EU and EAEU covering trade-related issues could be negotiated. This would entail elements of limited trade facilitation and further regulatory convergence. The EU and EAEU could also develop a political framework to state that the DCFTAs and EAEU are not in conflict and that their ultimate objective is to bring the *acquis* and EAEU norms closer together.[22] This could help diffuse the political tensions and the perception of either/or choices faced by the in-between states.

Third, the sides could negotiate a mutually acceptable trading framework for third countries that are not members of the EU or EAEU, and are not DCFTA signatories. This could be immediately applicable to Azerbaijan, if Baku is interested in such an arrangement. In the future, it could be adapted for countries that exit their current trading arrangements. For example, if a future Moldovan government decides to exit the DCFTA, it could adopt this proposed framework.

Finally, in the long term, the sides could discuss the potential for an EU-EAEU FTA.

Proposals for the In-Between States

We assume the current frameworks adopted by the in-between states—i.e., DCFTA agreements for Georgia, Moldova, and Ukraine, and EAEU membership for Armenia and Belarus—will remain in place, but could be adapted to allow for facilitated multidirectional trade. Such adaptations will, of course, differ in each case. We describe proposed adaptations below.

Georgia and Armenia

Georgia's and Armenia's experiences offer important examples for the other states. Given their current commitments, these countries have arrangements that allow for relatively effective multidirectional trade. Both have shown that it is possible to lean toward one side while not being cut off from the other. To be sure, Georgia might benefit from further formalization of its CIS FTA arrangements with Russia, particularly by including dispute resolution mechanisms. Armenia would also benefit from any future EU-EAEU arrangements. However, compared with the other in-between states, Georgia and Armenia have managed to achieve relative balance.

---

22 Here, the EAEU and the Chinese Belt and Road Initiative agreement on mutual compatibility could be instructive. A similar general agreement between the EU and EAEU—that their integration initiatives are not in conflict—could help reduce tensions.

Belarus

For Belarus, a CEPA with the EU would be desirable, replicating Armenia's experience. A necessary first step, however, would be to finalize Belarus's WTO accession. The WTO's Working Party on the Accession of Belarus was established in 1993, and, after a long period of inactivity, it resumed its activities in January 2017. The most recent consultations took place in July 2019.[23]

Moldova and Ukraine

Georgia's arrangements with Russia could be a model for Moldova and Ukraine; however, given Moscow's stated policies, there would need to be additional negotiations to ensure compatibility of trade relations in both cases. All sides (i.e., the two countries, the EU, and Russia and the EAEU) would need to be flexible and ready to make mutually acceptable compromises, consistent with their WTO obligations, their respective integration projects, and existing international agreements. A model for a process for adapting the DCFTAs can be found in another trilateral agreement among Brussels, Moscow, and third states: specifically, the talks that preceded the 2004 round of EU enlargement. As that process was being finalized, extensive negotiations occurred among the EU, Russia, and those East Central European countries joining the bloc (Czechia, Estonia, Hungary, Latvia, Lithuania, Poland, Slovakia, and Slovenia). EU negotiators took Russian concerns—which included issues such as aluminum exports to Hungary and a transit corridor to the Russian exclave of Kaliningrad (through Lithuania)—into account, and made adjustments in response.[24]

Resolving disputes regarding Ukraine's trading arrangements is particularly important. Russia has expressed concerns about the reexport of EU-produced goods to Russia by Ukraine. Additional measures, concerning rules of origin, could be considered to address these concerns, so that Moscow could return to implementation of the CIS

---

[23] WTO, "Accessions: Belarus," webpage, undated.

[24] European Union and the Russian Federation, "Joint Statement on EU Enlargement and EU-Russia Relations," press release, Luxembourg, April 27, 2004.

FTA in its trade relations with Ukraine.[25] Talks could generate credible commitments on mechanisms to address this concern, taking into account the parties' existing obligations. In addition, such talks could contribute to finding mutually acceptable solutions regarding DCFTA provisions that contradict particular CIS agreements. For example, Ukraine's obligations to adopt certain EU technical standards appear to contradict the 1992 CIS Agreement on Coordinated Policies in Standards, Metrology and Certification, which is mentioned in Article 11 of the CIS FTA as mandatory for signatories to implement.[26] Mutually acceptable compromises on these issues should allow Ukraine to return to free trade with Russia via the CIS FTA.

For normalizing trade relations with Moldova, Russia's central concern appears to be standards—in particular, with respect to Russian goods' market access after Chisinau decided to shift to EU standards.[27] In fact, Russia-Moldova negotiations on trade normalization, held in 2016, focused exactly on the issues of standards, phytosanitary measures, and certification.[28] In return for a negotiated solution on this matter, Moscow could fully normalize trade relations with Chisinau.

In addition, the EAEU could initiate negotiations with the DCFTA signatories on agreements similar to the one it reached with China in 2018.[29] This agreement provided for trade facilitation, but created no free trade area between the parties.

Azerbaijan

Azerbaijan currently seems to have limited ambitions for enhanced trade regimes with the EU and EAEU, given the dominance of hydrocarbons in its exports. However, since it is the only country in the

---

[25] It should be noted that the EU disagrees with Moscow on the necessity of additional measures to address reexport of EU goods via Ukraine.

[26] See Commonwealth of Independent States, 2011.

[27] Całus, 2014.

[28] "Foaia de parcurs, ca mijloc de normalizare a schimburilor comerciale cu Rusia," *Sputnik Moldova*, July 5, 2016.

[29] Eurasian Economic Commission, "Agreement Signed on Trade and Economic Cooperation Between EAEU and PRC," May 17, 2018.

region without preexisting obligations in this sphere, Azerbaijan presents an opportunity for the EU and EAEU to negotiate trade arrangements that are mutually acceptable. Baku, Brussels, and Moscow could begin talks through the trilateral mechanism described in the next section, with the goal of reaching such an agreement.

Summary

These patchwork solutions, even if successfully implemented, would not produce a seamless trade infrastructure for the region. Sadly, that is not a plausible medium-term goal. But they would represent a dramatic improvement over the status quo and allow all parties to benefit from normalized and, in some cases, enhanced multidirectional trading relations.

Trilateral Consultations

We propose that these efforts to find agreements on facilitating multidirectional trade be supplemented by permanent and comprehensive trilateral consultation mechanisms on issues related to the economic interests of the in-between states in their relations with the two blocs. For each nonmember of a Customs Union (Azerbaijan, Georgia, Moldova, and Ukraine), there would be a separate mechanism that would include officials from the EU, the EAEU, and the in-between state concerned.[30]

The primary goal of the trilateral mechanisms would be to both address short-term issues (such as disputes over phytosanitary standards) and consult on potential future changes to economic arrangements. Parties would commit to activating the mechanism and informing each other of changes to their trade regimes or other economic integration plans that might affect any of the other parties. Any party could raise an issue and seek consultation.

Apart from the official consultation mechanism, parallel nongovernmental trilateral groups should be established, involving both a business-to-business track and an expert track. These could be mod-

[30] Representatives of other organizations (such as the CIS) and states could join the mechanism to address a particular issue relevant to their competencies.

eled on the B20 and T20, the parallel business leaders and think tank summits that meet on the sidelines of the G20. They could devise solutions and propose them to governments directly or make their recommendations public. Consultations among business representatives and experts have a lower political profile than official consultations, and therefore could find more common ground. Over time, the nongovernmental groups might directly facilitate the official "first" track.

Norms Governing the Behavior of the Blocs

In addition to seeking agreements to iron out existing challenges and establishing permanent consultation mechanisms, both the EU and EAEU should commit to three norms governing their behavior in the region. First, to address concerns about revisionism, each bloc should accept the legitimacy of the other in its current composition. This would entail a political commitment not to "poach" the other bloc's members, encourage exits from the other bloc, or undermine its unity. Such a commitment would not affect the sovereign decisions of the member states, such as to leave one bloc or join another. But both sides would commit not to encourage such behavior or create other fissures. Emphasis should be placed on negotiation and engagement, recognizing the other bloc as a legitimate partner that should be treated like any of the other countless regional economic blocs that exist around the world.

Second, the EU and EAEU should commit to consulting on future significant changes to trade and economic arrangements in the region. Specifically, both blocs should pledge to discuss and, when possible, seek mutual consent for major new initiatives, including potential future institutional enlargement, giving due weight to regional stability and the economic interests of all parties. This norm would help avoid situations when one bloc could be blindsided by the other's policy shifts. It should be noted that EU enlargement entails much more than just economic integration; it involves commitments in the political, legal, and security domains, *inter alia*. However, given existing EU decisions noting that the Association Agreement "does not confer . . . the status of a candidate country for accession to the Union, nor does it constitute a commitment to confer such status . . . in the future," it should be possible to commit to consulting prior to changing such decisions.[31]

Third, both blocs should recommit to respecting in-between states' current economic integration choices—that is, not to induce them to choose one bloc or exit current arrangements—so long as they reach mutually acceptable arrangements for multidirectional trade and consult on future changes through the trilateral mechanism. In other words, assuming compromises are reached to address existing trade issues, Russia would renounce ambitions for Georgia, Moldova, and Ukraine to join the EAEU, and the EU would accept that future trade ties with Armenia and Belarus would be mediated through their status as EAEU members—barring future changes in those states' preferences. The in-between states would retain their sovereign right to change their policies in the future, of course, but this commitment would ensure that any changes would be made without external pressure.

Such norms would limit friction and unnecessary misunderstandings (and minimize the securitization of economic policies) but would not limit the choices of nonmember states. Taken together with the multidirectional trade arrangements and trilateral consultation mechanisms, these norms should create strong incentives to refrain from the practice of economic coercion that has become commonplace in the region.

Conclusion

Improvement of the economic arrangements for in-between states can contribute to and benefit from progress on the two other elements of the dispute over the regional order—the security architecture and regional conflicts. But this element is critical in itself, given the economic and political significance of recent disputes surrounding trade regimes. Our proposals would lead to functioning multidirectional

---

[31] European Council, "Conclusions of the European Council Meeting," memorandum, December 15, 2016.

trade relations among all countries in the region and create norms and mechanisms to avoid future disputes. If implemented, these measures would reduce the likelihood that economic relations would become a source of conflict and would facilitate the prosperity of the in-between states, thus creating incentives to address the other elements of the regional order.

CHAPTER FOUR

Regional Conflicts

Samuel Charap, Vasyl Filipchuk, Ulrich Kühn, Andrei Popov, Nikolai Silaev, Olesya Vartanyan

Any future effort to revise the regional order in post-Soviet Europe and Eurasia must address the region's protracted conflicts. For the states affected by them, the conflicts represent their most significant security concern and a core component of their domestic politics. For the region as a whole, the conflicts restrict trade, increase social hardships, weaken governance, heighten tensions, and limit people-to-people ties. At the international level, the disputes surrounding the status of conflict zones and the presence of third parties there frequently lead to deadlock in multilateral talks. Many Western states view a change in the dynamics surrounding the conflicts—and specifically Russian behavior—as a prerequisite to engagement in a broader discussion on the regional order. Russian officials, in turn, have argued that Western approaches to the conflicts must be transformed to achieve regional stability.

A revised regional order must therefore deliver concrete progress on the conflicts. It will be impossible to address the other disputes over the security architecture and economic integration without parallel steps on the conflicts.

This chapter proposes an interlinked framework to address the conflicts: Relevant parties involved would agree to implement a series of steps to improve the lives of the people affected by the conflicts and reduce tensions on the ground, while simultaneously making a renewed commitment to pursue a settlement that is supported by all parties. Such a framework would entail concrete steps toward alleviating the consequences of the conflicts, while providing affected states enhanced confidence that multilateral negotiation formats will operate with renewed purpose. Such a framework cannot guarantee results, but the trade-off is clear: In return for facilitating a normalization of the situation on the ground, conflict-affected states would receive a strong political commitment from relevant parties (e.g., the United States, Russia, the European Union [EU] and its key member states, and the Organization for Security and Co-operation in Europe [OSCE]) to reinvigorate efforts to reach a mutually agreed settlement.

Our proposal assumes that the other two elements of the dispute over the regional order—the security architecture and economic integration, or geopolitics and geoeconomics—are being addressed in parallel processes, with significant progress being made and the prospect of success in finding a mutually acceptable agreement seeming plausible to the key parties. In other words, the set of instruments we propose are intended to be implemented in a regional context that is fundamentally different from today's because of the atmosphere created by these parallel talks. We assume that the three negotiating processes will have to take place in parallel for them to be successful; our proposals are intended for a potential future window of opportunity that does not exist today.

We should also be clear what this chapter does *not* address. We do not critique or debate the merits of the current negotiating formats or existing agreements regarding the conflicts. We are not proposing solutions that could be implemented if today's level of geopolitical conflict persists. We also avoid specific recommendations relevant to specific conflicts as much as possible. Our intention instead is to describe a mutually acceptable framework for addressing this central element of the dispute over the regional order.

The rest of this chapter proceeds as follows. First, we analyze the linkages between the conflicts and the other two elements of the contestation over the regional order. Some have argued that progress must be made on incremental achievements in the negotiations addressing one or more of these regional conflicts before beginning discussions on the other two issues. While such small steps forward are certainly possible in theory, our analysis demonstrates that in practice they will remain tenuous, reversible, and limited barring parallel efforts on the other tracks, particularly on the security architecture. We show that current conditions—when the security architecture and economic integration issues are intensely contested—pose specific, significant roadblocks to both conflict management and, particularly, settlement. The tracks have become too deeply intertwined to be addressed in isolation. We also describe how progress on the other two tracks would provide direct benefits for conflict management.

There are also those who claim that the regional conflicts would disappear if enough progress was made on the geopolitical dispute, so that external sponsorship of separatist movements would cease. But the second section demonstrates that there are other dynamics, in addition to those related to the other regional disputes, that drive the conflicts. It therefore makes clear that a specific process will be necessary to address the conflicts.

We then describe our proposed framework for what such a process could entail. This framework would consist of a bargain that links more-effective conflict management to a renewed international commitment to talks on settlement. We lay out two menus of potential conflict-management measures that could be taken, covering those that reduce the suffering of conflict-affected populations and those that lower military tensions and the risk of armed clashes. We also describe principles of status neutrality that should be observed, so that states can implement these measures without crossing established redlines, even if those states have fundamental disagreements.

Conflict-affected states would be loath to take these measures without some hope of achieving negotiated settlements of the disputes. Therefore, the management process we propose would be linked to intensified international efforts to find mutually agreed settlements. We describe a number of principles that should be observed in the talks. The final section discusses additional incentives that can be provided for states and entities to engage in this process. These include reconstruction assistance and potential withdrawal of forces.

Interlinkages Between the Other Two Elements of the Regional Order Dispute and the Conflicts

Although the majority of the regional conflicts began largely because of intergroup or political disputes, they have all become entangled (if to varying degrees) with the geopolitical and geoeconomic clashes between Russia and the West. This linkage is central to understanding both recent history and the prospects for future improvements. Observers and official mediators often decry the lack of progress achieved in the various negotiation formats created to address the conflicts. Indeed, even modest steps toward more proactive, multilaterally endorsed conflict-management measures—let alone conflict settlement—have been relatively rare, despite much hard work from the diplomats and officials involved. This dynamic, we contend, is fundamentally driven by the linkage between the conflicts and the other two aspects of the regional order. Under the current circumstances, steps toward settlement *or even effective conflict management* have potential costs in those two other domains that outweigh any potential benefits of such steps for key actors. Why would a party agree, for example, to improve humanitarian access to a conflict zone, if doing so might compromise its broader security interests? States have few incentives to agree to conflict management steps, even concerning issues that seem unrelated to settlement, given the linkages to broader disputes. The following section describes how the status quo limits current efforts at conflict management and how agreement on the geopolitical and geoeconomic level could facilitate such efforts.

How the Status Quo Limits the Effectiveness of Conflict Management

There are a range of mechanisms through which the current geopolitical and geoeconomic disputes over the regional order limit the realm of the possible when it comes to effectively managing the conflicts, or moving toward settlement. One basic mechanism is clear: Russia has little incentive to agree to settlements that could increase the prospects of further enlargement of Euro-Atlantic institutions. But the following are additional roadblocks that the current disputes create:

- Which nations contribute to a potential peacekeeping force for the regional conflicts immediately gets tied to the underlying geopolitical dispute. The relevant external actors are all believed to prioritize their geopolitical competition over effective peacekeeping. For example, in Nagorno-Karabakh, the parties have repeatedly refused to agree to a peacekeeping mission, in part to avoid further projection of the geopolitical competition onto the conflict.[1]
- Conflict management is currently seen as furthering Russia's agenda, because it reinforces a status quo that is unacceptable to other parties. Many in Tbilisi, for example, believe that steps toward normalization of life on the ground in the conflict zones make the situation more sustainable and thus prolong what they believe to be an unacceptable status quo.[2] High geopolitical tensions thus reduce incentives for states and entities, in certain cases, to engage with Russia on conflict management.
- The current level of geopolitical confrontation amplifies the threat perceptions of some regional states by creating the sense of being caught in the cross fire of great-power competition. Increased threat perceptions, in turn, decrease willingness to engage in humanitarian efforts.
- The prospect of membership in Euro-Atlantic institutions creates a rationale for elites in aspirant countries not to engage in reconciliation or other conflict management efforts. Integration with or membership in the EU or the North Atlantic Treaty Organization (NATO) is viewed by many in these countries as a shortcut to conflict resolution. The argument is that the sheer magnetic pull that the states can create, via Euro-Atlantic integration, will make those on the other side of the conflict lines forget their fears,

---

1 Thomas de Waal, "Prisoners of the Caucasus: Resolving the Karabakh Security Dilemma," Carnegie Europe, June 16, 2016.

2 For example, this has led to restrictions on the work of international nongovernmental organizations—including humanitarian organizations—in the entities where there is conflict. See Sabine Fischer, "The EU's Non-Recognition and Engagement Policy Towards Abkhazia and South Ossetia," Brussels: EU Institute for Security Studies, December 2010.

grievances, and aspirations and thus seek unconditional reincorporation.[3]

- As a result of the broader confrontation with Russia over regional order issues, Western policymakers are loath to provide explicit incentives for regional states to engage in conflict management. Doing so, some argue, would be akin to giving Russia a veto over Western engagement with regional states.[4]
- Geopolitical discord has weakened key multilateral institutions that have a mandate to manage conflicts, most importantly the OSCE and the Council of Europe. The organizations have become battlefields in the geopolitical clash, thus dramatically limiting their effectiveness to respond to crises and conflicts.[5]
- Geopolitical tensions have been a key factor in driving escalatory spirals on the ground that have led to war, and thus the total breakdown of conflict management. For example, the dispute over Georgia's NATO aspirations during and after the April 2008 NATO Bucharest summit contributed to the tensions that precipitated the war that came less than four months later.[6]
- Equally, the geopolitical tensions create incentives for states to escalate on the ground to shape bargaining processes on the international level.
- The geoeconomic competition over trade regimes in the region further complicates cross–conflict line commerce.[7]

---

[3] For example, when then–Georgian Prime Minister Irakli Garibashvili signed his country's Association Agreement with the EU, he appealed to "my brothers and sisters—Abkhazians and South Ossetians," explaining to them that they "have the unique opportunity to enjoy benefits provided by the association with Europe." The implicit assumption appears to be that "association with Europe" will obviate the need for societal reconciliation. "Georgia, EU Sign Association Agreement," *Civil Georgia*, June 27, 2014.

[4] The following publication makes this case for Georgia: Damon Wilson, *Georgia's Path to NATO*, Washington, D.C.: Atlantic Council, February 2014, p. 2.

[5] Regarding the impact on the OSCE, see Stefan Lehne, *Reviving the OSCE: European Security and the Ukraine Crisis*, Washington, D.C.: Carnegie Endowment for International Peace, September 22, 2015. A partial exception has been the OSCE's Special Monitoring Mission in Ukraine.

[6] See Charap and Colton, 2017, pp. 93–94; and Thomas de Waal, *The Caucasus: An Introduction*, Oxford, UK: Oxford University Press, 2010, pp. 208–209.

[7] In Georgia, particularly, this has been the case.

Positive Spillover from the Other Two Tracks for Conflict Management and Settlement

Just as the status quo impedes steps forward on the conflicts, progress on the other two tracks would facilitate more-effective conflict management and improve the prospects of finding mutually agreed settlements. Specifically, movement toward agreement on the geopolitical and geoeconomic disputes would provide all parties incentives to engage on the conflicts. These incentives include the following:

- Moscow would have far greater incentive to allow conflict negotiations to progress if norms regarding further enlargement of regional security institutions were to be negotiated in parallel. Currently, the only way for Russia to stop the movement of Euro-Atlantic structures toward its borders is to raise the costs of doing so, including via the existing conflicts; that would no longer be the case if the dispute over the security architecture were to be addressed.
- With the lessening of regional tensions, there would be far greater political space for multilateral agreement on conflict-management measures, ranging from peacekeeping to education, infrastructure, medical, and other humanitarian efforts. Currently, these measures are either blocked because of the tensions or, if they exist, limited in effectiveness because they are not agreed to by all parties.
- If geopolitical tensions were relieved through the parallel negotiations on the security architecture, the major powers and relevant international organizations could be far more effective, proactive, and coordinated in their conflict mediation efforts.
- If disputes over economic integration were resolved to mutual satisfaction, there would be more opportunities for cross-boundary trade and commerce.
- If geopolitical tensions were eased, states would have more incentive to remove barriers to cross-boundary people-to-people communication.
- Diminished tensions create greater incentive for regional states and entities to be constructive and cooperative regarding conflict-

related issues, because there would no longer be any need for them to signal loyalty to their patrons by taking a hard-line approach. In other words, the current dynamic—whereby certain states and entities can act as "proxies" for the opposing sides in the geopolitical clash—would dissipate significantly, if not cease completely.

- Equally, with progress on the geopolitical track, outside powers would be more willing directly to incentivize constructive behavior regarding the conflicts.
- It is possible that steps toward resolution of the geopolitical dispute could diminish the relative role of hard-power instruments and increase the use of soft-power approaches, particularly for Russia. Once national security concerns are no longer driving policy, Russia's reputation in the region will become a more important consideration in its decisionmaking, making it less likely for Moscow to resort to coercive measures.
- Lowering the level of geopolitical confrontation through the talks would diminish parties' incentives to attempt to impose on one another their divergent positions on territorial disputes. Indeed, one can imagine creative efforts to move forward on conflict management *despite* disagreement over the status of disputed territories under these circumstances. There would likely be more room to negotiate frameworks for interactions among entities and central governments.
- Diminishing the existing geopolitical tensions could have a major impact on the domestic politics of the states of the region. It could lessen domestic political polarization and empower moderates. The states in the region would be more likely to prioritize economic development over security. With moderates in power, internal political reforms that facilitate settlement, such as decentralization, would be more likely.

Regional Conflicts Go Beyond Geopolitics

The preceding section documented the linkages between the conflicts and the geopolitical and geoeconomic elements of the regional order dispute. However, the conflicts in post-Soviet Europe and Eurasia would not just disappear if those elements were addressed.[8] There are drivers of the conflicts that do not relate to the disagreements over the security architecture and economic integration. Therefore, a process will be necessary to address the protracted conflicts.

The global experience of conflict mitigation and resolution demonstrates that a mere end to external support for one side of the conflict does not lead to societal reconciliation. Conflict is often sustained by political grievances and intergroup tensions, particularly if the conflict involved significant violence. In other words, easing the international-level disputes would not necessarily resolve the conflicts' internal drivers. The conflict in and over Nagorno-Karabakh is an apt example. There is relatively little divergence in Russian and Western policies on the conflict. Even during the peak of the Ukraine crisis in 2014, Russian, French, and U.S. diplomats (the three countries are the cochairs of the OSCE Minsk Group, the main negotiation platform on the conflict), including at the ministerial level, have succeeded in finding common ground on Nagorno-Karabakh.[9] But the conflict persists and it is almost impossible for the parties to make steps toward sealing a peace deal.

While grievances partly explain the persistence of the Nagorno-Karabakh dispute (and, indeed, the other conflicts in the region), there is an additional level of contradiction between the sides both there and elsewhere: deeply divergent narrative frameworks regarding the conflict. Donald Horowitz termed such a contradiction a "metaconflict" in his analysis of ethnic and racial fragmentation and political cleavages in South Africa.[10] Horowitz argued that, in addition to the race-

---

8 An assumption that the reverse is true, it should be noted, is prevalent in much discussion of the conflicts: For example, some in Kyiv argue that the Donbas conflict would be instantaneously resolved if Russia withdrew support for the armed insurgency.

9 See, for example, OSCE, "Joint Statement by the Heads of Delegation of the OSCE Minsk Group Co-Chair Countries," December 4, 2014. See also Sergey Markedonov, "A Post-Soviet Anomaly: How Karabakh Could Bring Russia and the West Together," Carnegie Moscow Center, October 10, 2017.

10 Donald L. Horowitz, *A Democratic South Africa? Constitutional Engineering in a Divided Society*, Berkeley, Calif.: University of California Press, 1991, p. 27.

related conflict itself, the contradictory explanations and visions of that conflict contributed to the divisions in South African society and impeded reconciliation:

> South Africa [is] a society divided along ideological lines—lines that demarcate fundamental differences in how the society ought properly to be understood and organized. Whereas in other settings knowledge about a society can proceed cumulatively, in South Africa virtually every interpretive effort involves some return to first principles, even to first facts.

Therefore, he concluded, there is

> not one conflict in South Africa, or even one type of conflict, but two. There is the conflict itself, and there is the metaconflict—the conflict over the nature of the conflict. Neither is coterminous with the other; neither can be reduced to the other.[11]

Notwithstanding the significant differences between the South African and the post-Soviet conflicts, similar metaconflicts—the conflict over the nature of the conflict—are present throughout the region.

In the conflicts in post-Soviet Europe and Eurasia, we can see not only a clash between contradictory and incompatible state-building and nation-building projects and corresponding versions of historical memory, but also deep discursive contradictions on what Horowitz termed "first principles" and "first facts." We can see fierce disputes over the nature of the conflicts, such as how to define the parties (for example, the difference between "separatists" and "puppets"), the sources and driving forces of the conflicts, how and when the conflicts began, and what prevents resolution. For example, the dominant narrative among Georgians holds that Abkhaz and South Ossetian separatism in the late 1980s and early 1990s was initiated and supported by the Soviet and then Russian governments. By contrast, most Abkhaz and South Ossetians believe their conflict was with the Georgian government, a government which, they believe, was supported

---

[11] Horowitz, 1991, pp. 1–2.

by Moscow.[12] While academics have extensively studied the struggles over contested interpretations and understandings of groups and their relations to "others," politicians and political observers often do not recognize that this discursive level of conflict is at least as important as its "material" reality.[13]

The degree of metaconflict in the region varies significantly. The opposing narratives of the Nagorno-Karabakh conflict are very influential and deeply embedded in the life of the respective societies.[14] Perhaps this is unsurprising, given the depth of the mutual grievances in that case. But even in cases where the level of grievances is low, we can detect the metaconflict. In Moldova, for example, interpretative frames of the Transnistria conflict differ significantly. Some see the conflict as a clash between Romanian nationalists who seek to "reunite" Moldova with Romania and forcefully assimilate Transnistrians, while others see the breakaway region as an instrument of Russian policy being used to undermine an emerging democracy.

The metaconflict does not only affect the parties to a given conflict. The contestation between different explanations and interpretations of the same events influence those who attempt to mediate as well. Whether consciously or unconsciously, mediators contribute to the metaconflict with their implicit positions or by the proposals they offer. It is almost impossible for third parties to be truly neutral when a metaconflict exists, and it is even harder to be perceived by the sides as neutral.

---

12 See S. K. Zhidkov, *Brosok maloi imperii*, Maikop, Russia: Adygeya, 1996.

13 See, *inter alia*: V. A. Shnirelman, *Voiny pamyati: mify, identichnost' i politika v Zakavkaz'e*, Moscow: Nauka, 2003; Paul R. Brass, *Theft of an Idol: Text and Context in the Representation of Collective Violence*, Princeton, N.J.: Princeton University Press, 1997; and Rogers Brubaker, *Ethnicity Without Groups*, Cambridge, Mass.: Harvard University Press, 2004.

14 For example, see Larisa Sotieva, Arda Inal-Ipa, Jana Javakhishvili, and Liana Kvarchelia, *Envisioning Peace: An Analysis of Grassroots Views on the Nagorny Karabackh Conflict*, London: International Alert, October 2018.

Proposal, Part I: Conflict Management

Even if there were to be agreement among the key players on the other two elements of the regional order, the grievances that drive the conflicts would not disappear, and thus the conflicts themselves would likely persist. A process would therefore be necessary to address them. The remainder of this chapter describes our proposal for such a process. It would involve negotiations to agree on more-effective conflict management, a renewed commitment to find mutually agreed settlements, and incentives for the parties to engage in the process. This section describes proposed measures for conflict management, grouped under the rubrics of pain reduction and confidence- and security-building measures (CSBMs). To implement our proposal, standing negotiation platforms will be necessary for both the management and settlement tracks. The composition of these groups will of course differ for each specific conflict. But the central point is that all steps would be agreed among the key parties. The prospect for mutually agreed measures is what differentiates this process from most current efforts regarding the conflicts today and what offers a chance for a better outcome.

Pain-Reduction Measures

We use the term *pain-reduction measures* to refer to steps that reduce human suffering associated with the conflicts. That in itself is a worthy objective, but pain reduction is also important for creating incentives for constructive engagement in a conflict settlement process. A recent large-*N* study suggests that increased pain among conflict-affected populations creates greater instability.[15] Pain-reduction measures can thus create micro-level understandings that facilitate broader negotiations. They can help transform intergroup dynamics, build trust and interdependence, and create a more conducive environment for conflict settlement. Over time, they can even reduce the underlying diver-

---

[15] See Halvard Buhaug, Lars-Erik Cederman and Kristian Skrede Gleditsch, "Square Pegs in Round Holes: Inequalities, Grievances, and Civil War," *International Studies Quarterly*, Vol. 58, No. 2, 2014.

gences in narratives and mutual grievances by regularizing interaction among once-estranged populations.

Pain-reduction measures are present to some extent in the region today (see the appendix for a description of the measures that have been implemented by the governments of Georgia, Moldova, Armenia, and Russia). These examples demonstrate that some steps are possible even under the current adverse political conditions. However, the limited nature of the existing measures also demonstrate how those conditions dramatically limit the realm of the possible.

A number of lessons can be distilled from the current practice of pain-reduction measures in the region:

- Pain-reduction measures have had a positive impact on the lives of local populations, even if there is little noticeable effect on the prospects for conflict settlement.
- Territorial disputes and associated status claims limit effective implementation of pain-reduction programs.
- The programs themselves are limited in scope because of lack of engagement (let alone mutual agreement) among the regional states, Russia, and the de facto authorities. For example, Georgian efforts to allow Abkhazia-based firms to take advantage of the Deep and Comprehensive Free Trade Area agreement have faltered, because the Abkhazian authorities refuse to engage on the subject.
- The legitimacy of current pain-reduction measures is often called into question because not all relevant actors are involved in devising them.

Table 4.1 summarizes the categories of pain-reduction measures currently in place in the region and includes a range of more-ambitious measures. Many measures currently possible in one conflict zone are unimaginable in another. Under different political circumstances, however, much more ambitious measures could be possible in all the region's conflicts. Table 4.1 is a menu from which parties can select the measures most relevant to a given conflict and adapt them to the par-

Table 4.1
Potential Pain-Reduction Measures for Regional Conflicts

Economic	Humanitarian	People-to-People
Integration of road and rail networks	Easing boundary-crossing procedures	Access to central government's education system for residents of conflict zones
Investment in development projects	Pension and salary payments for residents of conflict zones	Access to national sports team for athletes from conflict zones
Support for international companies' operations in conflict zones	Provision of medical care for residents of conflict zones	Access to national cultural competitions (e.g., Eurovision)
Mutual recognition of license plates	Recognition of local identification documents	Support for residents of conflict zones to participate in international scholarship programs
Establishment of trade corridors across conflict lines	Permitting international organizations and third countries to support civil society development in the conflict zones	Participation in national elections for conflict-zone populations
Application of international economic agreements in conflict zones	Granting international humanitarian access to conflict zones	Refraining from enacting bans on websites and social media based in the conflict zones
Access to national banking system for residents of conflict zones	Technical assistance for mitigating the risks of landmines and other postconflict reconstruction	Allowing third-country citizens to transit through conflict zones
Access to national power grid for conflict zones	Support to local medical personnel and facilities in conflict zones	

ticular circumstances thereof. Not all measures will be applicable to all conflicts, of course.

The fundamental difference between the pain-reduction measures present today and those to be implemented according to our proposal would be that they would be agreed to by all the relevant parties by definition. Many of the existing pain-reduction measures described in the appendix are essentially unilateral: They result from the initiative of one party without the buy-in or, in some cases, even the consent of other relevant parties. This dynamic inherently limits their legitimacy and effectiveness, since the parties that have not bought in to these measures have an incentive to undermine them. Our proposal calls for multilaterally agreed pain-reduction measures, or to give the existing measures greater legitimacy through their endorsement by all relevant parties. This would likely significantly enhance the effectiveness of such measures, or at the very least remove obstacles to their effectiveness.

These pain-reduction measures—in addition to political reconciliation efforts, youth engagement across conflict lines, and peace-centered education efforts—offer the only realistic prospect, over time, of addressing the metaconflicts and intergroup divisions that currently exist in the region's conflict zones. Without them, the microdrivers of conflict will endure.

CSBMs

In addition to pain-reduction measures, more-effective conflict management would entail a reduction in tensions among the parties and an improvement in the security situation on the ground.[16] Today, in many of the region's conflict zones, unpredictability, insecurity, and misperceptions thrive, creating significant risks of renewed or intensified fighting. Measures to reduce those risks could help to better manage the conflicts.

---

[16] This section builds on Sergi Kapanadze, Ulrich Kühn, Wolfgang Richter, and Wolfgang Zellner, *Status-Neutral Security, Confidence-Building and Arms Control Measures in the Georgian Context*, Hamburg, Germany: Institute for Peace Research and Security Policy, CORE Working Paper No. 28, January 2017.

There are a number of such measures already present in the region today:

- In Georgia, the European Union Monitoring Mission (EUMM) operates a "hotline" for the Georgian government, the Russian military, and the de facto authorities to resolve incidents.[17]
- The United Nations (UN) and the OSCE convene Incident Prevention and Response Mechanisms for the Abkhazia and South Ossetia conflicts, respectively.[18]
- The EUMM has rights to inspect Georgian military and police facilities near the conflict lines.[19]
- Georgia unilaterally agreed to limit the number of forces and quantity of certain military equipment deployed within a specified area along the conflict lines. Tbilisi also provides notification of all deployments to that area and of any military exercises greater than battalion strength. This information is conveyed by the EUMM to the authorities in the entities and the Russian military commanders on the ground.[20]
- The OSCE Special Monitoring Mission in Ukraine has hundreds of monitors who report on cease-fire violations.[21]
- There is a joint peacekeeping force in Moldova.[22]

Our proposal is to introduce more effective and comprehensive CSBMs, endorsed by all the relevant parties. The general purpose of reducing the risk of armed conflict should be to increase mutual security and predictability, thereby helping to improve the living condi-

---

[17] EUMM Georgia, "Georgia: Hotline of the EU Monitoring Mission Helps to Prevent Conflicts," June 18, 2018.

[18] EUMM Georgia, "93rd IPRM Meeting Takes Place in Ergneti," May 16, 2019.

[19] EUMM Georgia, "EUMM Enhances Co-Operation with the Georgian Minister of Internal Affairs," May 27, 2009.

[20] Samuel Charap and Cory Welt, *A More Proactive U.S. Approach to the Georgia Conflicts*, Washington, D.C.: Center for American Progress, February 2011, p. 26.

[21] OSCE, "OSCE Special Monitoring Mission to Ukraine," webpage, undated.

[22] See Ministry of Defense of Moldova, "Peacekeeping Missions," webpage, undated.

tions of all people affected by the conflict. Respective measures could include different elements of communication, transparency, or restraint (see Table 4.2).[23]

We propose that the following two principles should guide implementation of the CSBMs:

- **Reciprocity:** Any CSBMs should contain at least a modicum of reciprocity. Reciprocity should not be conflated with "equality" in a political or legal sense. Rather, it refers to all parties to a conflict adopting appropriate measures of communication, transparency, or restraint as outlined in Table 4.2, as opposed to one party doing so and others not. Ideally, measures would be applied in the same way to all sides; for example, limitations on deployments to specific geographical areas would be of comparable size. However, in certain cases, perfect mirroring might not be possible; the key is that all sides adopt measures of significance to the others.
- **Dispute management:** Mechanisms to manage disputes would be established to ensure effective implementation. Preexisting formal or informal formats that deal, for example, with the implementation of cease-fire agreements could be tasked with this responsibility, or new institutions could be established. Such a mechanism would include an impartial third-party mediator or convener and the parties to the conflict. It would be charged with consultation and clarification of questions regarding implementation of and compliance with specific CSBMs, consultation and clarification about incidents or concerns about unusual military activities, or immediate response measures to crisis situations.

More-advanced risk-reduction measures could also be introduced; for example, insertion of a peacekeeping operation (PKO) into the conflict zone, particularly if the parties to a conflict are unable to ensure an effective cease-fire (despite declaring their commitment to stop violence). An authorized PKO could be deployed to facilitate a cease-fire

[23] The measures described in Table 4.2 are meant as a general illustration of the variety of potential options available. Measures are not listed in any specific order.

Table 4.2
Potential CSBMs to Reduce Risks in Conflict Zones

Communication	Transparency	Restraint
• Designated points of contact (PoCs) for military matters • Military-to-military hotlines • Consultation regarding unusual military activities • Consultation and cooperation on hazardous incidents of a military nature • Development of shared definitions of military equipment, force structures, and geographic areas • PoCs and consultations for notifications, information exchange, observations, demonstrations, hosting, and inspections • Specific provisions for clarification of concerns and evaluation of compliance with agreements • Regular meetings of dispute-resolution bodies	• Prior notification of certain military activities • Notification of increases in armed personnel • Notifications of plans for acquisition and deployment of major weapon and equipment systems • Exchange of lists of existing types of certain heavy military equipment • Exchange of information about holdings of major weapon systems and those newly entered into service • Exchange of information about command structure, personnel, or equipment holdings with specific levels of disaggregation • Demonstration of new types of major weapon systems • Third-party monitoring of incidents and agreements (e.g., cease-fire, withdrawal) • Transparency measures on surplus small arms and light weapons (SALW) • Observation procedure for certain military activities or specified areas • Voluntary observation visits to dispel concerns about military activities • Inspection of certain military installations, particularly in sensitive areas	• Withdrawal zones for certain heavy military equipment • Limitations on certain military equipment in specified areas • Limitations on the number of armed forces deployed in specified areas • Limitations on certain military activities in specified areas • Limitations on quantity of SALW in specified areas • Refraining from enacting bans on websites and social media based in the conflict zones • Allowing third-country citizens to transit through conflict zones • Destruction of excess military equipment • Demining • Establishment of demilitarized zones • Limiting numbers of certain military activities in specified areas (e.g., exercises) • Demobilization of certain armed forces • Reduction of overall national holdings of certain equipment or numbers of personnel

and even to enforce it. The PKO would be based on the UN Charter and international best practices, including the invitation of the host country and the parties to the conflict. To be efficient, the PKO has to have a clear mandate; sufficient human, administrative, technical, and financial resources; clear goals; and a time frame for the achievement of those goals. If the parties to the conflict mutually agree, a PKO can include not only military components but also police and civilian elements. Subject to mutual agreement, a PKO could include not only peacekeeping but also peacebuilding activities, such as engaging local populations in bridge-building and reconciliation projects. A PKO could facilitate disengagement of military units of the sides, return of heavy weapons to storage facilities, and even conducting voluntary buy-back programs enabling collection of small arms that are in possession of the local population. An international mission can also conduct verification of demilitarization of the conflict areas, in cooperation with local and central authorities. A PKO might not be appropriate for all conflicts, but it should be considered along with the other conflict-management measures described above.

Ensuring Status Neutrality

Throughout the region, parties hold conflicting positions regarding the status of a particular territory in or near the conflict zones. Certain parties might consider a conflict zone to be a region of a particular country; others might consider it to be an independent state or part of a different country. The issue of status is central to the conflicts; it has also consistently proven to be a major roadblock for more-effective conflict management, since the parties either use the measures to reinforce their status claims or worry that another party might do so. To take just one example, the EUMM is prevented from operating in Abkhazia and South Ossetia because its mandate includes the phrase "in Georgia," and neither Russia nor the authorities in the entities recognize their territory as part of Georgia.

Even if there were shared political will to pursue enhanced conflict management, agreeing on concrete measures would still be difficult because of the very nature of regulating such measures. Whoever consults on, devises, or implements measures bears ownership and responsibility, and thus a certain form of authority. Authority can convey status, and status—in both a political and a legal sense—is one of the most disputed issues in the conflicts. De facto authorities in disputed territories that lack international recognition or status can become *status seekers* (i.e., they seek recognition of their status claims) because such recognition would grant them legitimacy. However, central governments that lack effective control of disputed territories—but claim sovereignty over those territories—will go to extreme lengths to prevent that outcome, and thus can become *status spoilers*; in other words, they spoil seemingly unrelated processes to reinforce their positions on status. To take an example from outside the region, the Republic of Cyprus regularly blocked EU engagement with Turkey because of the status dispute with Ankara over northern Cyprus.[24] Third-party states that recognize the independence of a disputed territory often attempt to act as *status enablers* by actively supporting the de facto authorities in their quest for recognition.

De facto authorities categorically reject the right of the governments from which they seek to separate to act on their behalf on all issues pertaining to the territory they control, including for purposes of implementing conflict-management measures.[25] These authorities typically either want to exercise such rights themselves or to deny that the disputed territory belongs to the area of application of the agreement in question if the central government is the signatory. Third-party states that have *not* recognized de facto authorities are not permitted, under international law, to act in contravention to the central government's position on the status of disputed territories. The situation gets more complicated if a third-party state *has* recognized the independence of a disputed territory, since that adds international legal disputes into the mix.

Under our proposed new framework for conflict management, the states involved would commit to negotiating instruments to reduce

---

[24] See James Ker-Lindsay, "The Policies of Greece and Cyprus Towards Turkey's EU Accession," *Turkish Studies*, Vol. 8, No. 1, 2007.

[25] See, for example, "Abkhazia, South Ossetia Alarmed by Russia-Georgia WTO Compromise," Radio Free Europe/Radio Liberty, November 27, 2011.

pain and lower the risk of conflict without seeking to undermine each other's respective status claims. The following principles would be observed:

- **No ill intent:** Negotiations would begin with a mutual commitment not to use the talks or the measures that might result from them to further any party's status claims, and an acknowledgment that implementation of any agreed measures would not affect any state's position on status. This would neutralize concerns that conflict-management measures could lead to "creeping recognition" of one party's status claims.
- **Third-party facilitation:** A third party (i.e., not one of the parties to the conflict) would be involved in the process of negotiating measures from the onset. The third party could be a state or group of states not directly involved in the conflict, an international organization, or even a private enterprise. That third party could assist in the process of convening conflict parties to craft status-neutral measures. Once conflict parties agree on certain measures, arrangements could take on the form of nonlegal documents signed by the third party and the conflict parties—separately, if necessary, to avoid privileging one side's position on status.
- **Status-neutral designations:** Agreements on conflict-management measures would avoid any designations that contain direct or indirect references to statehood, sovereignty or related concepts, institutions, titles of persons, or geographical names. Instead of geographical names, GPS coordinates could serve as identifiers of territory. Instead of using titles of persons involved in talks, they could be referred to only by their name as written in a mutually agreed language, perhaps other than the official language(s) of the conflict parties.
- **Status-neutral terminology and procedures:** International agreements usually use terminology and procedures that might

be deemed to privilege one party's position on status.[26] Such terminology can be avoided by using GPS coordinates and agreed generic terms. Status-neutral procedures would entail entrusting a third party with the implementation of conflict-management measures and communication among conflict parties.

Proposal, Part II: Moving from Conflict Management Toward Settlement

The preceding sections described our proposal for measures to address the humanitarian and security challenges created by the regional conflicts. These measures would become possible were the disputes over the security architecture and economic integration to be addressed in parallel processes. However, even if successfully implemented, these status-neutral pain-reduction and risk-reduction steps would not, in themselves, constitute a path toward settlement. (Moreover, effective pain-reduction measures and CSBMs could, in principle, be implemented without a prospect of settlement.)

Our proposal is to link adoption of more-comprehensive conflict-management measures—pain reduction and risk reduction—to a renewed international commitment to negotiate settlements to the conflicts. This commitment would be made by the states affected by or involved in the conflicts, other countries that have participated in negotiations to date, and the major international organizations engaged in the conflicts (e.g., the EU, OSCE, UN). The normalization of the situation on the ground—achieved through effective conflict management—would create fertile ground for the talks, making the international commitment more than just rhetorical.

The status quo of contested borders and disputed status is suboptimal for all states involved. Therefore, if the political conditions are propitious, activation of negotiations to reach mutually acceptable outcomes should be a commitment they all can make. Moreover, sev-

---

[26] Such as *inspecting/inspected/host state, escort team, national points of entry/exit, national visa requirements*, and so forth.

eral of the region's conflicts are interlinked in such a way as to make true "freezing" (i.e., no bloodshed or threat of use of force, but no settlement) nearly impossible; tensions in one conflict zone can spill into another. Any settlements that do arise from this process would be highly specific to the circumstances of the respective conflicts. However, we suggest that the parties commit to the following general principles to guide the talks:

- **Mutual consent:** A true settlement is only possible with the consent of all the relevant parties.
- **Peaceful settlements only:** The parties renounce the use of force to resolve the conflict and commit to a peaceful settlement process.
- **Interconnected tracks:** Parties cannot expect settlement to proceed if management is blocked and vice versa. The process cannot end at the management phase or jump to settlement without effective management in place.
- **Open-ended negotiations:** By open-ended, we mean that negotiations cannot succeed if parties enter the talks unwilling to accept anything less than achieving their maximalist objectives. The parties need to be open to accepting a range of possible outcomes from the talks.
- **Respect for the rights of the displaced:** Parties commit to the principle that the rights of internally displaced persons and refugees should be respected, even if the form in which those rights would be realized could vary.
- **Economic reconstruction:** For those areas that suffered during the "hot" phase of the conflicts, any settlement should provide for reconstruction assistance.
- **Restorative justice:** A commitment to a public process to facilitate societal reconciliation without retribution. This usually takes the form of a truth and reconciliation commission to document past injustices and human rights abuses and create a permanent public record. Over the past three decades, more than 40 countries have established truth commissions. Such restorative justice

processes are focused more on healing society's wounds rather than the retributive justice of war-crimes tribunals.

Proposal, Part III: Additional Incentives for Regional States and Entities to Engage

To reiterate, the fundamental bargain contained in our proposal is twofold. First, the parties should adopt a more proactive and effective framework for conflict management, choosing from the range of measures presented above. Second, the states involved should make a commitment to finding a mutually acceptable framework for settlement according to the principles outlined in the previous section. This proposal inherently provides incentives for all sides to engage.

However, some might argue that certain states would be making perceived concessions on conflict management, while getting only a political commitment to achieve settlement, which, we acknowledge, is not a guarantee. We propose that the major powers and international organizations involved in the regional conflicts consider the following additional measures to increase incentives for conflict-affected states and entities to engage:

- **Reconstruction assistance:** The EU, the United States, and Russia could pledge significant funds to pay for reconstruction as part of this process.
- **Economic carrots and sticks for entities:** States can provide additional economic stimulus or apply conditionality for aid in return for the entities' cooperation with the conflict-management and settlement processes.
- **End to conflict-related sanctions:** Many economic sanctions have been imposed on states in the context of the conflicts. These sanctions could be relieved in return for engaging in the process.[27]

---

[27] We are referring to, for example, the closure of the border between Turkey and Armenia.

- **Outside powers withdraw forces:** NATO member states and Russia could negotiate mutual reductions of the scale of military presence and activities in and near conflict zones.

Provision of these incentives to regional states and entities should be conditioned on their willingness to engage in the conflict-management and -settlement program proposed above. If they are unwilling to engage, they should not be able to benefit from these incentives.

Conclusion

The regional conflicts are tightly interlinked with the other two elements of the dispute over the regional order. Parallel progress on the security architecture and economic integration would make possible a range of steps forward on the conflicts that, barring such progress, would be completely impossible. Therefore, steps forward on the other two tracks would, in themselves, hugely benefit the situation surrounding the regional conflicts. But even if there were to be progress on those tracks, the regional conflicts would not disappear. Substantive measures will be necessary both to better manage them and to provide some prospect of finding a settlement. The three-part proposal we offer here—enhanced, multilateral, status-neutral conflict-management measures to reduce pain and risk, combined with a renewed international commitment to finding settlements and incentives to engage in the process—provides the tools to improve the situation on the ground in the short term and lays the groundwork for settling these disputes. Progress on the conflicts along these lines will in turn be critical for facilitating the talks on the other two tracks.

CHAPTER FIVE

Summary: A Consensus Proposal for a Revised Regional Order

Samuel Charap

The preceding three chapters have described a multifaceted proposal for a revised regional order. The proposed revision would create a new consultative body for major-power engagement on the regional security architecture, new norms governing the behavior of the blocs, and a status offering for nonaligned states. It would entail tailored solutions to facilitate multidirectional trade; establish regular dialogue among the European Union (EU), Eurasian Economic Union (EAEU), and in-between states; and create new norms regarding the trade blocs' behavior. Finally, it would launch linked efforts to move forward on status-neutral management measures for the regional conflicts and on mutually agreed settlements. See Box 5.1 for a more detailed outline of the three interlinked pieces of the proposal.

This proposal will not completely satisfy any party; agreeing to it would require difficult compromises from all. But if implemented, it would represent a dramatic improvement over the status quo. It would end the negative-sum competition for the loyalty of the in-between states. Major powers would cease actions that threaten the security and prosperity of these states. And there would be real progress on addressing the regional conflicts. Moreover, no state would be required to cross declared red lines to achieve this outcome. The proposal therefore represents a potentially viable political compromise, one that could significantly increase stability and reduce insecurity in the region and, more broadly, provide guardrails to the Russia-West competition.

Box 5.1
The Proposed Revised Regional Order

Security Architecture

- *Regional security consultations (RSC)*: Regular consultations will be held to discuss the regional security architecture, address any disputes regarding it, and provide mutual reassurance about intentions. Permanent participants are the United States, Russia, and the EU; any in-between state can convene a meeting of the RSC and be heard.
- *Norms of behavior:* Permanent participants in RSCs agree not to seek further changes in the composition of existing regional security institutions or in the geopolitical status of current alliance members without consultations and attempts to find mutual consensus, giving due weight to regional stability and the security interests of all parties. Any state adopting the third-way status would commit to consulting with the permanent participants if it chooses to change its security arrangements in the future.
- *Third-way status:* A nonaligned state could seek a third-way status that would entail explicit acknowledgment of its nonalignment and recognition of that status by the major powers.
- *Multilateral security guarantees (MSGs) and confidence- and security-building measures (CSBMs):* Third-way status is reinforced by formalized multilateral security guarantees to those states that adopt it. In addition, the major powers agree to make those guarantees meaningful through a series of military-restraint and transparency measures that would demonstrate their commitment to the third-way states' security.

Economic Integration

- *Multidirectional trade relations:* The parties would create functioning and mutually beneficial trade regimes for in-between states with both the EU and the EAEU. The specific arrangements would include
  - EU-EAEU arrangements, such as harmonization of technical regulations and deconflicting transit issues; a framework agreement between the EU and EAEU; a mutually acceptable trading framework for third countries that are not members of the EU or EAEU and not Deep and Comprehensive Free Trade Area (DCFTA) agreement signatories; and, eventually, an EU-EAEU free trade area agreement
  - tailored solutions for each in-between state to allow for functioning trade relations with both the EU and the EAEU, taking into account their respective obligations under existing agreements (e.g., the DCFTAs or EAEU membership provisions).
- *Trilateral consultations:* The parties commit to the creation of comprehensive trilateral consultation mechanisms on issues related to the economic interests of the in-between states in their relations with the two blocs. For each nonmember of a Customs Union (Azerbaijan, Georgia, Moldova, and Ukraine), there would be a separate mechanism, including officials from the EU, the EAEU, and the in-between state concerned.
- *Norms of behavior:* The EU and the EAEU agree to accept the composition and the legitimacy of existing institutions; consult on significant changes to the status quo as concerns trade and economic arrangements in the region; and respect in-between states' integration choices.

Regional Conflicts

- *Enhanced conflict management:* Parties will adopt a much more proactive approach toward managing the regional conflicts. This would include
  - pain-reduction measures, which are steps that reduce human suffering associated with the conflicts
  - CSBMs, steps that reduce the risk of armed conflict and improve the security situation on the ground
  - a commitment to status neutrality, wherein the states involved commit to negotiating these instruments without seeking to undermine each other's respective status claims.
- *Recommitment to conflict settlement:* Affected and involved states, alongside other countries and organizations that participated in prior negotiations, make a renewed international commitment to negotiate settlements to the conflicts and principles to govern the settlement process.
- *Incentives to engage:* Third-party states provide the conflict-affected states with incentives to engage in the process, such as generous economic reconstruction packages.

Comparing the proposed revised regional order with the status quo in detail is important to appreciate the differences between the two fully. (These are summarized in Table 5.1.) In terms of the security architecture, the region today is essentially fractured between two competing blocs. Whereas the proposed order creates a mechanism for regular consultation regarding the regional security architecture, today there is essentially no government-to-government dialogue on this subject involving the major powers and the in-between states. The North Atlantic Treaty Organization (NATO)–Russia Council is moribund. Organization for Security and Co-operation in Europe (OSCE) meetings have largely devolved into recitations of mutual grievances. If the alignment of an in-between state were to be called into question today,

Table 5.1
Comparison of the Status Quo with Proposal for a Revised Regional Order

	Status Quo	Proposal
Security architecture	• Dysfunctional dialogue mechanisms or ones that do not address the problems • No observed norms for bloc and major-power behavior toward in-between states • Status choices of in-between states contested by major powers • No credible security assurances for nonaligned states • Increased major-power military activity affecting in-between states	• RSCs bring together the key actors to address the problems causing regional instability • Agreed norms to govern major-power behavior and preclude unilateral decisions • Third-way status offer provides nonalignment with major power buy-in • Third-way states provided effective multilateral security guarantees • Major powers exercise military restraint toward third-way states and vice versa
Economic integration	• Either/or integration choices • Disrupted trade patterns because of clash of integration projects • No bloc-to-bloc or trilateral dialogue or essentially dysfunctional dialogue • No observed norms of behavior for the blocs	• Facilitated multidirectional trade via EU-EAEU arrangements and tailored solutions for the in-between states • Establishment of trilateral consultation mechanisms for the nonmembers of blocs • Agreement not to undermine existing institutions and in-between states' choices and to consult about any future changes
Regional conflicts	• Limited conflict management, much of it unilateral, often hijacked by disputes over status • Negotiation processes on settlements without high-level political investment from major powers or any hope of success • No incentives for constructive engagement	• Enhanced, multilateral status-neutral conflict-management measures for pain and risk reduction • A renewed international commitment to negotiate settlements • An incentive package for all affected parties to engage in the process

both Russia and the West would likely act to achieve outcomes unilaterally and potentially coercively without even notifying the other side, let alone consulting. Today, fears abound that one of the major powers is seeking to undermine the other side's bloc by encouraging exits; alternatively, some decisionmakers are convinced that one or the other major power seeks geopolitical domination in the region at all costs. This zero-sum dynamic creates insecurity for all.

Rather than universal buy-in for the status of the in-betweens, essentially all three categories (nonaligned, Russian-aligned, and Western-leaning) are, to some degree, contested by one or more of the major powers. Nonaligned Azerbaijan and Moldova are objects of major-power competition, if only because neither Russia nor the West believes that the other side respects their nonalignment. Russia's allies cannot develop normal ties with the West without engendering Moscow's suspicions, which are not so far-fetched. And NATO and the EU have consistently refused to grant the explicit choices of Western-leaning Ukraine and Georgia to become members of those organizations, while at the same time offering just enough partnership to engender Russian retribution.

Under the proposed revised order, major-power disputes over the status of the in-between states would be resolved cooperatively through the RSC. Russia and the West would commit to make changes to the security architecture through a process of mutual consultation. Efforts to undermine the existing blocs would cease. Those states that adopt the proposed third-way status would reap significant security benefits from the security guarantees and related restraint measures.

Economic ties in the region today are contested and under strain. The competition between incompatible trade regimes has led to disrupted commerce and created either/or integration choices for the in-between states. Moldova and Ukraine are implementing DCFTA agreements with the EU, but face major barriers in trade with Russia. The lack of formal barriers in trade between Russia and Georgia has been tenuous, since these arrangements are under-institutionalized and subject to political perturbations. There are no dialogue mechanisms in place among the EU, EAEU, and the in-between states to address these issues. Meanwhile, the lack of explicit agreement on norms of behavior between Moscow and Brussels leaves both sides with the impression that the other seeks to undermine its interests, an impression that is often based in fact.

Under the proposal in this volume, economic ties would be restored through a series of arrangements aimed at facilitating multidirectional trade. The EU and EAEU would negotiate accords to facilitate the position of the in-between states—those that are DCFTA signatories, those that are members of the EAEU, and Azerbaijan. Tailored solutions for each in-between state would address current problems, removing restrictions on trade with all major partners and offering opportunities for enhanced ties with both blocs. Regular trilateral consultation mechanisms would be established for all nonmembers of the blocs with representatives of both groups to address any future concerns. And Brussels and Moscow would make normative commitments to reassure each other and the in-between states.

In terms of the regional conflicts, the current situation is quite grim, despite the best efforts of diplomats involved in the process. The conflict-management efforts that do exist are modest at best, and most of them are unilateral, hobbled by disputes over status, or both. As a result, the security situation on the ground is tenuous, particularly as concerns human security. The extant negotiation formats have, in some cases, been meeting for over two decades with little movement toward settlement. Moreover, certain important actors have little incentive to take any political risk to achieve progress on the conflicts.

Under the proposal in this volume, a comprehensive conflict-management program, negotiated through inclusive multilateral talks, would be implemented. It would include a selection from the menu of pain- and risk-reduction measures described in Chapter Four, as appropriate for each particular conflict. These measures will have explicit guarantees of status neutrality to prevent any party's red lines from being crossed. This conflict management push would be linked to a new international commitment to find settlements. Although no promises on outcomes would be made, assurances of political investment in the process would make this new commitment more than mere rhetoric, and explicit economic and political incentives would be provided to all parties to engage.

It is important to note that these three components of the regional order must be addressed in parallel to achieve the outcomes described. If one piece falls away, the others will fall with it. They are interlinked components of the current dispute, and, therefore, the solutions must be interlinked.

These ideas are deliberately not meant to be one-size-fits-all for the six in-between states, which differ in many key respects. The proposal in this volume can therefore be adapted to address the in-between states' particular circumstances, threat perceptions, and security challenges with tailored solutions. It is important to underscore that our proposals are aimed equally at improving the plight of the in-between states, as they are at better managing the competition between Russia and the West. In Table 5.2, we compare the status quo regarding the three components of the regional order dispute as they affect each in-between state, and the situation that could result if the proposal described here were adopted. Table 5.2 demonstrates that our proposals indeed offer significant benefits for each of the six countries.

The changes in the regional order that we propose would not be easy to implement and would entail costs. Indeed, our proposal is likely to be highly politically charged.[1] But the situation today is suboptimal for all parties. All relevant capitals need to start the process of thinking about alternatives. The proposal offered here provides one vision for a way forward. The most important change required today is to begin to have an open discussion about these thorny issues. Barring that, an already bad situation will only continue to deteriorate.

[1] That said, polling data indicate that there is significant support for compromises on at least the security architecture and economic integration pieces in five of the in-between states. See Charap, Shapiro, and Demus, 2018, pp. 34–36.

Table 5.2
Comparison of the Status Quo with the Proposed Revised Regional Order for the In-Between States

	Status Quo	Proposal
Ukraine	• NATO aspirations without realistic prospect of membership • EU DCFTA; trade with Russia cut off; no ongoing trilateral talks • War raging in Donbas; little short-term hope for effective management or settlement	• Multilateral security guarantees; major-power buy-in for nonalignment and greater restraint[a] • DCFTA and restored trade with Russia; standing trilateral consultation mechanism • Implementation of status-neutral pain-reduction measures and CSBMs; renewed settlement process
Georgia	• NATO aspirations without realistic prospect of membership • EU DCFTA; trade with Russia tenuous; no trilateral talks • Conflicts with minimal management and practically no settlement prospects	• Multilateral security guarantees; major-power buy-in for nonalignment and greater restraint[a] • DCFTA and institutionalized trade regime with Russia; standing trilateral consultation mechanism • Implementation of status-neutral pain-reduction measures and CSBMs; renewed settlement process
Belarus	• Collective Security Treaty Organization (CSTO) membership, but Moscow wary of any ties with the West • EAEU membership; links with EU limited by being out of the World Trade Organization (WTO), lack of EU-EAEU ties • Negative indirect security repercussions from regional conflicts, particularly Donbas	• Reduced tensions and increased stability surrounding current and future status • EAEU membership and WTO membership, Comprehensive and Enhanced Partnership Agreement (CEPA)–like agreement with EU; trade with EU bolstered by EAEU-EU deals • Reduction in security risks because of better conflict management

Table 5.2—Continued

	Status Quo	Proposal
Azerbaijan	• Nonalignment without acknowledgment from major powers • No enhanced trade regimes with either EU or EAEU • Conflict with practically no management measures or settlement prospects	• Multilateral security guarantees; major-power buy-in for nonalignment and greater restraint[a] • Potential for mutually compatible arrangements with both EU and EAEU • Implementation of status-neutral pain-reduction measures and CSBMs; renewed settlement process
Armenia	• CSTO membership, but Moscow wary of any ties with the West • EAEU membership and CEPA with EU; links with EU limited by lack of EU-EAEU ties • Conflict with practically no management measures or settlement prospects	• Reduced tensions and increased stability surrounding current and future status • Status quo plus enhanced links with EU via new EAEU-EU arrangements • Implementation of status-neutral pain-reduction measures and CSBMs; renewed settlement process
Moldova	• Nonalignment without acknowledgment from major powers • EU DCFTA; trade with Russia limited; no ongoing trilateral talks • Conflict with modest management measures but practically no settlement prospects	• Multilateral security guarantees; major-power buy-in for nonalignment and greater restraint[a] • DCFTA and restored trade with Russia; standing trilateral consultation mechanism • Implementation of status-neutral pain-reduction measures and CSBMs; renewed settlement process

[a] We assume, for this comparison, that Moldova, Azerbaijan, Ukraine, and Georgia adopt the proposed third-way status. It is important to acknowledge that this would require a voluntary decision to change current policies.

APPENDIX

Current Pain-Reduction Measures in the Region

Olesya Vartanyan, Andrei Popov, Nikolai Silaev

Georgia

After the 2008 war and Russia's recognition of Abkhazia and South Ossetia, Georgia introduced a dual approach to its policy toward those entities. On the one hand, it maintains a policy of nonrecognition, demanding the withdrawal of the Russian military and restoration of its control over the entities. The main goal has been to prevent what some call the "creeping recognition" of Abkhazia and South Ossetia by any foreign states or actors.[1] The law on occupied territories declared illegal any unauthorized contacts with the authorities there and established a restrictive framework for travel and economic interactions with Abkhazia and South Ossetia.[2] On the other hand, Georgia promotes an engagement policy for the people living in Abkhazia and South Ossetia, declaring readiness to respect the rights of and provide support to those who accept Tbilisi's legal authority.[3]

---

1 Interviews conducted by Olesya Vartanyan with former and current senior officials in the Georgian government, October 2018.

2 Parliament of Georgia, Law of Georgia on Occupied Territories, No. 431, October 23, 2008. For a critical review of the law, see European Commission for Democracy Through Law, Final Opinion on the Draft Amendments to the Law on Occupied Territories of Georgia, Strasbourg, France, Opinion No. 552, December 14, 2009.

3 Georgia's first engagement programs were revealed in the 2010 package, which included future-oriented long-term policy guidance for the rest of the Georgian state apparatus. See Office of the State Minister for Reintegration of the Republic of Georgia, "Action Plan for

The Georgian leadership faces political challenges to its engagement policy. Programs receive attacks and fierce criticism from opposition politicians and opinionmakers.[4] Every time the Georgian leadership relaxes the rules, it faces a storm of skepticism and criticism from inside the government and political opponents.

Georgian officials argue that every third person in Abkhazia and South Ossetia has either come to Tbilisi-controlled territory for services, or has a relative or a friend who has done so.[5] People are able to receive services that otherwise are not provided, either inside the entities or in Russia. This has helped to establish more people-to-people contacts and lessen the gap between the divided societies, which have been living apart for over two decades, since the first wars in the 1990s. There are several ongoing engagement projects today.

Pensions and Salaries

Georgia's ministries responsible for education and health institutions have special funds to cover expenses in Abkhazia and South Ossetia. Only those Abkhazians and South Ossetians with official Georgian documents have access to the Georgian banking system. Most of those individuals are school and hospital employees in eastern Abkhazia and the Akhalgori district of South Ossetia, both of which have a signifi-

---

Engagement," July 2010. Initially, a condition for participation in many of these projects was acceptance of the so-called neutral documents issued by the Georgian justice ministry. But this demand was later lifted and replaced with a more flexible approach, which started accepting the documents issued by the de facto Abkhaz and South Ossetian authorities.

4 For example, see the public debate over medical assistance to the people from breakaways that emerged in the public space in 2017: Tornike Sharashenidze, "Why Georgia's Abkhazia Policy Has Failed," *Civil Georgia*, October 5, 2017; Giorgi Kanashvili, "He Who Says A Must Say B—or Why Tornike Sharashenidze's Abkhazia Policy Fails," *Civil Georgia*, October 13, 2017; Ucha Nanuashvili, "Helping the Abkhaz, Ossetians Is Georgia's Obligation," *Civil Georgia*, November 20, 2017.

5 Interviews conducted by Olesya Vartanyan with one former official and one currently serving senior official in the Georgian government, October 2018. It was impossible to verify these numbers independently. Georgia does not publicize some of the statistics for those who took part in the engagement programs.

cant ethnic Georgian population. Many of them receive salaries from Abkhazian or South Ossetian authorities in parallel.[6]

Medical Assistance

The medical assistance program has been one the most successful products of the engagement strategy. From 2012 through 2016, more than 4,000 people, mainly from Abkhazia, received approximately $4 million worth of free medical assistance from the Georgian government. Before, the medical program targeted patients with acute issues and those who could not travel to Russia for treatment. Now, many patients visit Georgian hospitals for regular medical checkups.[7]

The absence of adequate medical facilities in Abkhazia and South Ossetia drives the popularity of this program. Although larger cities and towns might have newly renovated medical buildings, few have the professionals and medical equipment necessary to provide adequate services.[8] Travel to Russia and other foreign countries for local residents is often impossible because of the cost.[9]

Trade

Cross–conflict line trade also has provided economic opportunities for populations on both sides. Trade between Abkhazia and South Ossetia and Tbilisi-controlled territory has never stopped—even during the wars and military escalations—and is currently on the rise. Trade happens despite legal restrictions prescribed in the laws of Georgia and both entities.[10] Business is mainly conducted by local residents with

---

[6] Interviews conducted by Olesya Vartanyan with former senior Georgian government officials, October 2018, and interviews with residents of Abkhazia and South Ossetia, 2010–2019.

[7] Interview conducted by Olesya Vartanyan with senior Georgian government official, June 2018.

[8] For more details, see Thomas Hammarberg and Magdalena Grono, *Human Rights in Abkhazia Today*, Stockholm, Sweden: Olof Palme International Center, July 2017, pp. 43–46.

[9] In 2018, Russia started accepting Abkhazians and South Ossetians into its state insurance program, which includes free medical treatment.

[10] For more details, see International Crisis Group, *Abkhazia and South Ossetia: Time to Talk Trade*, Brussels, Europe Report No. 249, May 24, 2018, pp. 4–11.

connections on both sides of the dividing lines and is alleged to involve officials, who also profit from the unregulated processes.

Since 2015, trade with South Ossetia has been booming. Long lines of minibuses with cargo have been observed near the main crossing point leading to Akhalgori, where the population is largely ethnically Georgian. Around 1,500 tons of products entered the region every month during the summer of 2017.[11] Trade with Abkhazia is conducted through well-established networks. According to the Abkhazian authorities, 150 tons of commercial cargo cross the conflict line daily, in both directions.[12] The annual value ranges from $7 to $15 million, according to studies conducted from 2010 to 2015. Meanwhile, Georgia's "A Step for the Better Future" package seeks to allow Abkhazian businesses to use the Georgian free trade agreement with the EU by registering their businesses in Tbilisi-controlled territory.[13]

A key problem facing the implementation of trade initiatives is the lack of coordination between authorities on both sides and the main stakeholders. There is no conversation going on between the Georgian and Abkhazian or South Ossetian representatives. In Abkhazia, Sukhumi has not accepted the EU's invitation for mediation with Tbilisi on trade issues. Georgia's attempts to engage with Abkhazian authorities have not led to the establishment of a channel to discuss possible prospects for development of trade.

Education

The majority of international institutions do not recognize Abkhazian and South Ossetian education documents and request additional papers to confirm their validity. The Georgian government has recently proposed inviting a neutral international institution to coordinate the verification process with the Georgian government.[14] Additionally,

---

[11] International Crisis Group, 2018, p. 6.

[12] International Crisis Group, 2018, p. 8.

[13] International Crisis Group, 2018, p. 12.

[14] Office of the State Minister of Georgia for Reconciliation and Civic Equality, *"A Step to a Better Future": Peace Initiative, Enhancing Educational Opportunities for the Residents of Abkhazia and Tskhinvali Region/South Ossetia*, Tbilisi, Georgia, 2018a.

Tbilisi has supported the British government in its decision to introduce status-neutral terminology to allow residents of Abkhazia to apply for scholarships to attend graduate school in the UK.[15]

Documents

The primary barrier to including residents of Abkhazia and South Ossetia in Tbilisi-managed programs is related to identification documents. Tbilisi refuses to accept documents issued by the local authorities and instead has asked residents to apply for Georgia-issued papers. Since 2013, Georgia has relaxed some its regulations and allowed Abkhazian and South Ossetian passports to be used for registration purposes. This decision coincided with an increase in the numbers of people from the two entities applying for medical assistance in Georgian hospitals, as discussed in a prior section. Georgia's 2018 "A Step for a Better Future" program allowed Abkhazian and South Ossetian documents to be used to generate a state identification number, which can be used for a range of state and private services, including opening bank accounts and registering companies.[16]

Moldova

Since 2007, Moldova's policy toward a Transnistrian settlement has been based on engagement, small steps, and confidence-building. It was developed as a comprehensive, complex, and consistent policy supported by Moldova's key international partners, after almost two decades of incoherent and contradictory efforts, and a zig-zag trajectory when periods of soft and indulgent measures and initiatives were abruptly followed by restrictive and tough measures and frozen relations.

---

[15] Interviews conducted by Olesya Vartanyan with former senior Georgian government officials, October 2018.

[16] Office of the State Minister of Georgia for Reconciliation and Civic Equality, *"A Step to a Better Future": Peace Initiative, Facilitation of Trade Across Dividing Line*, Tbilisi, Georgia, 2018b.

After the July 2009 elections in Moldova, the new government formed by the Alliance for European Integration suspended the policy of isolating or ignoring Transnistria and launched a new policy of engagement.[17] Leaving aside difficult political issues, such as Transnistria's status, the government focused on small steps that could bring the sides closer to each other. It has tackled such issues as railways, economic cooperation, development projects (including social and health), and trade. A dozen working groups—ranging from economy, trade, and agriculture to health care, education, and environment—meet regularly.

Citizenship

Based on the provisions of the Moldovan law on citizenship,[18] a majority of Transnistrian residents are eligible for Moldovan citizenship, which has been granted to 330,000 residents (out of about 475,000 residing in the region), who received personal identification codes, internal identity cards, and international passports.[19] Of these, 288,000 are over 18 years old, and therefore can vote in Moldovan elections. Since 2005, Moldovan authorities have used a policy of positive discrimination toward Transnistrian residents, issuing their first internal identity document and first international passport free of charge (which costs the rest of Moldovan citizens seven euros and 45 euros, respectively).[20]

---

[17] European Commission, *Commission Staff Working Document, Accompanying the Communication from the Commission to the European Parliament and the Council, Taking Stock of the European Neighbourhood Policy (ENP): Implementation of the European Neighborhood Policy in 2009, Progress Report Republic of Moldova*, Brussels, May 12, 2010, p. 7.

[18] Parliament of the Republic of Moldova, Zakon Nr. 1024 ot 02.06.2000 o grazhdanstve Respubliki Moldova, August 10, 2000.

[19] "Nazvana chislennost' naseleniya Pridnestrov'ya," *point*, March 1, 2017.

[20] Government of the Republic of Moldova, Postanovlenie Nr. 959 ot 09.09.2005 o merakh po obespecheniyu podtverzhdeniya grazhdanstva i dokumentirovaniya naseleniya levoberezhnykh raionov Dnestra (Pridnestrov'ya), September 16, 2005.

Documents

Since May 2001, Moldova has de facto recognized and accepted the validity of the most types of documents issued in Transnistria.[21] Not only are these documents de facto accepted by Moldovan institutions, but some (such as civil registry documents and drivers licenses) can also be apostilled or transcribed into internationally recognized Moldovan documents, despite the fact that Chisinau authorities cannot access Transnistrian databases to verify their validity.

Medical Assistance

All Transnistrian residents who hold Moldovan citizenship (70 percent of the region's population) benefit from unlimited access to the Moldovan health care system with the purchase of a medical insurance policy (approximately 100 euros). Additionally, the Moldovan government issues thousands of free medical insurance policies for certain categories of Transnistrian residents, such as pensioners, disabled persons, and pregnant women every year. Moldova also allows residents of Transnistria to access medical programs targeting vulnerable groups and people with special needs.[22]

Education

The Moldovan Ministry of Education approves an annual quota of approximately 2,000 budget-supported seats in Moldovan universities that are reserved for graduates of Transnistrian schools. Because Transnistrian school education is 11 years and Moldovan is 12 years and a

---

[21] Oazu Nantoi, "Barter moldovenesc—suveranitatea declarata contra integritatii iluzorii," Institutul de Politici Publice, May 21, 2001; and Igor Boţan, *Reglamentarea transnistriană: o soluţie europeană*, Chisinau, Moldova: ADEPT, 2009a.

[22] See A. Efrim, "Polis dlya pridnestrovtsev," *Argumenty i fakti v Moldove*, March 20, 2013; and Government of the Republic of Moldova, "Guvernul a aprobat măsuri de susţinere a locuitorilor din regiunea transnistreană în vederea asigurării acestora cu medicamente antituberculoase şi antiretrovirale, precum şi cu dispozitive de diagnostic a tuberculozei şi a infecţiei HIV," July 25, 2018.

baccalaureate, Moldova organizes a free year-long transitional preparatory course for Transnistrians wishing to enter Moldovan universities.[23]

Car Plates

Since 2018, a mechanism for voluntary status-neutral car plates was approved that allows for the de facto acceptance of Transnistria-issued car plates on the entire territory of Moldova.[24] Now, Transnistrian car owners who wish to travel to the EU can be approved for Moldovan registration and status-neutral plates.

Transportation

In 2010, the Chisinau-Odessa-Tiraspol rail line resumed for the first time since the outbreak of the conflict and runs daily passenger trains from Chisinau to Odessa via Tiraspol.[25] In 2012, full-fledged freight rail service through the territory of Transnistria was restored.[26] Every year Chisinau and Tiraspol sign protocols reconfirming the legal basis for the cooperation in the field of train transportation, which envisages the unhampered passage through Transnistrian territory and the respective technical support for international trains coming from and to Moldova.

Travel Regime

The Moldovan government does not limit access to Transnistria for its citizens, either through the internal administrative line or from Ukraine. There are no customs or police checkpoints for cars entering the Transnistrian region from Moldova. To prevent smuggling, there

---

[23] Alla Ceapai, "Grigore Belostecinic: 'Mă bucură când îi aud pe cei veniţi din regiunea transnistreană spunând că vin la Chişinău pentru că aici e un nivel mai înalt al studiilor,'" Radio Europe Liberă Moldova, April 4, 2004.

[24] OSCE, "OSCE Mission to Moldova Welcomes Start of 'Licence Plate' Agreement Implementation by the Sides," September 1, 2018.

[25] "Poezda iz Ukrainy v Moldovu opyat' poedut cherez Pridnestrov'e," *ZN*, January 14, 2011.

[26] "Kishinev i Tiraspol' vozobnovili gruzovoe zheleznodorozhnoe soobshchenie cherez territoriyu Pridnestrov'ya, prervannoe 6 let nazad," *interlic*, April 26, 2012.

are, however, random checks for those vehicles entering Chisinau-controlled territory from Transnistria. In 2013, Moldova introduced mobile migration service posts at crossing points to register foreign citizens who enter the country via Transnistria.[27] There are no restrictions on foreign nationals who wish to access Transnistria from Chisinau-controlled territory.

Elections

All Transnistrian residents who hold valid Moldovan identification cards are eligible to participate in Moldovan parliamentary and presidential elections. The state register of voters for the February 2019 elections included 230,233 citizens residing on the territories controlled by the Transnistrian administration.[28] Tiraspol does not allow Moldovan parties to conduct electoral activities or to open polling stations on the territory it controls. However, between 6,000 and 10,000 Moldovan citizens living in Transnistria have historically traveled to Moldova proper to participate in elections.[29] In the second round of the 2016 presidential elections, this number doubled, reaching 17,000, while in the February 2019 parliamentary elections, an unprecedented number—37,000 voters—took part.[30]

Sport and Music

Moldova has maintained a single national championship team for all sports, in which Transnistrian teams and athletes may participate. Matches and competitions are held on both banks of the Dniester river. Transnistrian teams that often win or gain medals in Moldovan inter-

---

[27] "Moldova ustanovila shest' migratsionnykh postov v Zone bezopasnosti na Dnestre," webpage, undated.

[28] Comisia Electorală Centrală a Republicii Moldova, "Numărul total de cetăţeni cu drept de vot înscrişi în Registrul de Stat al Alegătorilor, la data de 10 decembrie 2018, este de 3 265 997," December 10, 2018.

[29] Igor Boţan, "Votul cetăţenilor Republici Moldova din regiunea transnistreană," *eDemocracy*, February 14, 2009b.

[30] Lina Grâu, "Vybory parlamenta i Pridnestrov'e," *Radio Europe Liberă Moldova*, March 4, 2019.

nal championships later participate as representatives of Moldova in various European championships. Singers and bands from Transnistria may also participate as representatives of Moldova in the Eurovision contest.

External Support from Russia and Armenia

In addition to actual or potential benevolent policies from Moldova or Georgia, such entities as Transnistria or Abkhazia enjoy support from external patrons. In the former Soviet Union, those patron states are Russia and Armenia. The patron state's aid helps the local population to survive and withstand pressure from the state that claims sovereignty over it. Such pressure varies in intensity and scale from conflict to conflict. It is rather low in the case of Transnistria, and extreme in the case of South Ossetia.

For decades the external patrons have provided public goods that can be seen as pain-reduction measures, even though the legitimacy of those measures is disputed by other parties, and the patrons have other nonaltruistic motives, such as reinforcing the entity's separation from the central government or maintaining the loyalty of local populations. These public goods include the following:

- Development of local infrastructure and reconstruction: Russia has spent significant sums developing roads and other infrastructure in several conflict zones. Moscow has also undertaken large-scale reconstruction programs in South Ossetia.[31]
- Economic and humanitarian aid: Russia provides direct economic assistance to Abkhazia and South Ossetia, providing over 50 percent of the former's and up to 90 percent of the latter's respective budgets.[32] It also plays an important role in economic

---

[31] Moscow committed $490 million in 2008 alone for reconstruction in South Ossetia. See "South Ossetia Becomes Thorn in Russia's Side," *Spiegel Online*, December 24, 2008.

[32] International Crisis Group, *Abkhazia: Deepening Dependence*, Brussels, February 26, 2010a; International Crisis Group, *South Ossetia: The Burden of Recognition*, Brussels, June 7, 2010b.

development in Transnistria.[33] State-led and nongovernmental organization–led humanitarian aid from Russia is indispensable for the populations in the nongovernment-controlled areas of Donetsk and Luhansk.[34]

- Social and health programs: Because many residents of conflict areas take the citizenship of the patron state, they are entitled to pensions and health care from the patron.
- Market access: In some cases, the external patron provides the only outlet for exports from conflict areas and thus helps local populations maintain their own economies. Armenia sells Nagorno-Karabakh's products in foreign markets and transfers collected taxes back to the region.[35]
- Education and developmental assistance: External patrons often educate populations of conflict areas in their own universities.[36]

These measures do reduce the pain of the local population, but they also change the incentive structure for the de facto authorities in conflict areas, particularly in their relations with the states that assert sovereignty over those areas. The patron's external aid increases the bargaining power of the de facto authorities, and can diminish the comparative value of pain-reduction measures offered by the states from which they seek to separate.

Future approaches to conflict management must take into consideration the external patrons' pain-reduction measures and the incentives they create. The challenge is how to make these measures part of

---

[33] As Kamil Całus writes, "Financial assistance received from Russia—both indirectly (so-called gas subsidies) and directly (humanitarian aid)—is . . . a key element which makes it possible for the Transnistrian economy to function" (Kamil Całus, "An Aided Economy: The Characteristics of the Transnistrian Economic Model," Center for Eastern Studies, May 16, 2013).

[34] Over 80 state aid convoys had been delivered to the Donbas by the end of 2018 ("Rossiya otpravila v Donbass novuyu kolonnu s gumanitarnoi pomoshch'yu," *RIA Novosti,* November 22, 2018).

[35] Interviews conducted by Olesya Vartanyan in Stepanakert, 2017–2018.

[36] For example, Asmat Tsvizhba, "Kvota na mechty: kak iz Abkhazii popast' v rossiiskii vuz," *Sputnik,* July 10, 2019.

a mutually agreed international framework supported by the regional states, de facto authorities, and the external patrons themselves. The external patrons will have to consider how to adjust their policies to create more incentives for the de facto authorities to engage in the conflict management and settlement processes.

References

"Abkhazia, South Ossetia Alarmed by Russia-Georgia WTO Compromise," Radio Free Europe/Radio Liberty, November 27, 2011. As of July 12, 2019: https://www.rferl.org/z/963/2011/11/27?p=3

Adarov, Amat, and Peter Havlik, *Benefits and Costs of DCFTA: Evaluation of the Impact on Georgia, Moldova, and Ukraine*, joint working paper, Vienna: Vienna Institute for International Economic Studies and Bertelsmann Stiftung, December 2016. As of July 11, 2019: https://wiiw.ac.at/benefits-and-costs-of-dcfta-evaluation-of-the-impact-on-georgia-moldova-and-ukraine-dlp-4111.pdf

Austria, France, Soviet Union, United Kingdom, and United States, Treaty for the Re-Establishment of an Independent and Democratic Austria, Vienna, May 15, 1955.

Boţan, Igor, *Reglamentarea transnistriană: O soluție europeană*, Chisinau, Moldova: ADEPT, 2009a. As of August 28, 2019: http://www.e-democracy.md/files/igor-botan-reglementarea-transnistreana.pdf

———, "Votul cetăţenilor Republici Moldova din regiunea transnistreană," *eDemocracy*, February 14, 2009b. As of July 12, 2019: http://www.e-democracy.md/monitoring/politics/comments/20090214/

Brass, Paul R., *Theft of an Idol: Text and Context in the Representation of Collective Violence*, Princeton, N.J.: Princeton University Press, 1997.

Broniatowski, Michał, "Tusk Makes Scathing Attack on Russian Influence," *Politico Europe,* October 6, 2018. As of August 28, 2019: https://www.politico.eu/article/donald-tusk-poland-russia-latvia-makes-scathing-attack-on-russian-influence/

Brubaker, Rogers, *Ethnicity Without Groups*, Cambridge, Mass.: Harvard University Press, 2004.

Buhaug, Halvard, Lars-Erik Cederman, and Kristian Skrede Gleditsch, "Square Pegs in Round Holes: Inequalities, Grievances, and Civil War," *International Studies Quarterly*, Vol. 58, No. 2, June 2014, pp. 418–431.

Całus, Kamil, "An Aided Economy: The Characteristics of the Transnistrian Economic Model," Centre for Eastern Studies, May 16, 2013. As of July 12, 2019: https://www.osw.waw.pl/en/publikacje/osw-commentary/2013-05-16/aided-economy-characteristics-transnistrian-economic-model

———, "Russian Sanctions Against Moldova: Minor Effects, Major Potential," Centre for Eastern Studies, November 6, 2014. As of July 12, 2019: https://www.osw.waw.pl/en/publikacje/osw-commentary/2014-11-06/russian-sanctions-against-moldova-minor-effects-major

Ceapai, Alla, "Grigore Belostecinic: 'Mă bucură când îi aud pe cei veniţi din regiunea transnistreană spunând că vin la Chişinău pentru că aici e un nivel mai înalt al studiilor,'" Radio Europe Liberă Moldova, April 4, 2004. As of July 12, 2019:
https://moldova.europalibera.org/a/25320526.html

Cenusa, Denis, Michael Emerson, Tamara Kovziridse, and Veronika Movchan, *Russia's Punitive Trade Policy Measures Towards Ukraine, Moldova and Georgia*, Brussels: Centre for European Policy Studies, CEPS Working Document, No. 400, September 2014.

Chalyi, Oleksandr, "Approaches to Resolving the Conflict over the States In Between," in Samuel Charap, Alyssa Demus, and Jeremy Shapiro, eds., *Getting Out from "In-Between": Perspectives on the Regional Order in Post-Soviet Europe and Eurasia*, Santa Monica, Calif.: RAND Corporation, CF-382-CC/SFDFA, 2018, pp. 33–38. As of September 9, 2019:
https://www.rand.org/pubs/conf_proceedings/CF382.html

Charap, Samuel, and Timothy J. Colton, *Everyone Loses: The Ukraine Crisis and the Ruinous Contest for Post-Soviet Eurasia*, Abingdon, UK: Routledge, 2017.

Charap, Samuel, Alyssa Demus, and Jeremy Shapiro, eds., *Getting Out from "In-Between": Perspectives on the Regional Order in Post-Soviet Europe and Eurasia*, Santa Monica, Calif.: RAND Corporation, CF-382-CC/SFDFA, 2018. As of September 4, 2019:
https://www.rand.org/pubs/conf_proceedings/CF382.html

Charap, Samuel, Jeremy Shapiro, and Alyssa Demus, *Rethinking the Regional Order for Post-Soviet Europe and Eurasia*, Santa Monica, Calif.: RAND Corporation, PE-297-CC/SFDFA, 2018. As of September 4, 2019:
https://www.rand.org/pubs/perspectives/PE297.html

Charap, Samuel, and Cory Welt, *A More Proactive U.S. Approach to the Georgia Conflicts*, Washington, D.C.: Center for American Progress, February 2011. As of July 12, 2019:
https://cdn.americanprogress.org/wp-content/uploads/issues/2011/02/pdf/georgia-report.pdf

Chivers, C. J., "A Russian 'Wine Blockade' Against Georgia and Moldova," *New York Times*, April 6, 2006. As of July 11, 2019: https://www.nytimes.com/2006/04/06/world/europe/06russia.html

Coffey, Luke, *NATO Membership for Georgia: In U.S. and European Interest*, Washington, D.C.: Heritage Foundation, Special Report No. 199, January 29, 2018. As of July 11, 2019: https://www.heritage.org/defense/report/nato-membership-georgia-us-and-european-interest

Comisia Electorală Centrală a Republicii Moldova, "Numărul total de cetățeni cu drept de vot înscriși în Registrul de Stat al Alegătorilor, la data de 10 decembrie 2018, este de 3 265 997," December 10, 2018. As of July 12, 2019: https://a.cec.md/ro/numarul-total-de-cetateni-cu-drept-de-vot-inscrisi-in-registrul-de-stat-al-alega-2781_91423.html

Commonwealth of Independent States, Treaty on a Free-Trade Area, St. Petersburg, Russia, October 18, 2011. As of July 11, 2019: http://www.eurasiancommission.org/ru/act/trade/dotp/sogl_torg/Documents/FTA%20CIS_Text_with_protocols_ENG.pdf

de Waal, Thomas, *The Caucasus: An Introduction*, Oxford, UK: Oxford University Press, 2010.

———, "Prisoners of the Caucasus: Resolving the Karabakh Security Dilemma," Carnegie Europe, June 16, 2016. As of July 11, 2019: https://carnegieeurope.eu/2016/06/16/prisoners-of-caucasus-resolving-karabakh-security-dilemma-pub-63825

"Dodon soobshchil, chto dogovorilsya s Putinym o tranzite moldavskikh tovarov cherez Ukrainu," TASS, January 30, 2019. As of August 28, 2019: https://tass.ru/ekonomika/6060358

Efrim, A., "Polis dlya pridnestrovtsev," *Argumenty i fakti v Moldove*, March 20, 2013. As of July 12, 2019: http://aif.md/polis-dlya-pridnestrovcev/

EUMM—*See* European Union Monitoring Mission in Georgia.

Eurasian Economic Commission, "Agreement Signed on Trade and Economic Cooperation Between EAEU and PRC," May 17, 2018. As of July 12, 2019: http://www.eurasiancommission.org/en/nae/news/Pages/17-05-2018-5.aspx

European Commission, *Commission Staff Working Document, Accompanying the Communication from the Commission to the European Parliament and the Council, Taking Stock of the European Neighbourhood Policy (ENP): Implementation of the European Neighborhood Policy in 2009, Progress Report Republic of Moldova*, Brussels, May 12, 2010. As of July 12, 2019: http://eeas.europa.eu/archives/docs/enp/pdf/pdf/progress2010/sec10_523_en.pdf

European Commission for Democracy Through Law, Final Opinion on the Draft Amendments to the Law on Occupied Territories of Georgia, Strasbourg, France, Opinion No. 552, December 14, 2009. As of July 12, 2019: https://www.venice.coe.int/webforms/documents/default.aspx?pdffile=CDL-AD(2009)051-e

European Council, "Conclusions of the European Council Meeting," memorandum, December 15, 2016. As of August 28, 2019: https://www.consilium.europa.eu/media/21929/15-euco-conclusions-final.pdf

European Union and the Russian Federation, "Joint Statement on EU Enlargement and EU-Russia Relations," press release, Luxembourg, April 27, 2004. As of July 12, 2019: https://library.euneighbours.eu/content/joint-statement-eu-enlargement-and-eu-russia-relations

European Union External Action Service, "New Agreement Signed Between the European Union and Armenia Set to Bring Tangible Benefits to Citizens," Brussels, November 24, 2017. As of July 11, 2019: https://eeas.europa.eu/headquarters/headquarters-homepage/36141/new-agreement-signed-between-european-union-and-armenia-set-bring-tangible-benefits-citizens_en

European Union Monitoring Mission in Georgia, "EUMM Enhances Co-Operation with the Georgian Minister of Internal Affairs," May 27, 2009. As of July 19, 2019: https://eumm.eu/en/press_and_public_information/features/1464/

———, "Georgia: Hotline of the EU Monitoring Mission Helps to Prevent Conflicts," June 18, 2018. As of July 12, 2019: https://eeas.europa.eu/headquarters/headquarters-homepage/46738/georgia-hotline-eu-monitoring-mission-helps-prevent-conflicts_en

———, "93rd IPRM Meeting Takes Place in Ergneti," May 16, 2019. As of July 12, 2019: https://eumm.eu/en/press_and_public_information/press_releases/6678/

Filipchuk, Vasyl, "What Should Be Ukraine's Position on Review of Regional Security Architecture," *Apostrophe*, August 28, 2019. As of August 28, 2019: https://apostrophe.ua/en/article/politics/2019-08-28/what-should-be-ukraine-s-position-on-review-of-regional-security-architecture/27564

Fischer, Sabine, "The EU's Non-Recognition and Engagement Policy Towards Abkhazia and South Ossetia," Brussels: EU Institute for Security Studies, December, 2010. As of July 11, 2019: https://www.iss.europa.eu/sites/default/files/EUISSFiles/NREP_report.pdf

"Foaia de parcurs, ca mijloc de normalizare a schimburilor comerciale cu Rusia," *Sputnik Moldova*, July 5, 2016. As of August 28, 2019: https://sputnik.md/moldova_romania_economics/20160705/7833285.html

"Georgia, EU Sign Association Agreement," *Civil Georgia*, June 27, 2014. As of July 12, 2019:
https://old.civil.ge/eng/article.php?id=27417

Gibler, Douglas M., *International Military Alliances, 1648–2008*, Vol. 2, Washington, D.C.: CQ Press, 2009.

Government of the Republic of Moldova, Postanovlenie Nr. 959 ot 09.09.2005 o merakh po obespecheniyu podtverzhdeniya grazhdanstva i dokumentirovaniya naseleniya levoberezhnykh raionov Dnestra (Pridnestrov'ya), September 16, 2005. As of September 5, 2019:
http://lex.justice.md/viewdoc.php?action=view&view=doc&id=305730&lang=2

———, "Guvernul a aprobat măsuri de susținere a locuitorilor din regiunea transnistreană în vederea asigurării acestora cu medicamente antituberculoase și antiretrovirale, precum și cu dispozitive de diagnostic a tuberculozei și a infecției HIV," July 25, 2018. As of July 12, 2019:
https://gov.md/ro/content/guvernul-aprobat-masuri-de-sustinere-locuitorilor-din-regiunea-transnistreana-vederea

Government of the Russian Federation, On the Introduction of Imported Customs Duties for Goods from the Republic of Moldova, Resolution No. 736, July 31, 2014, as amended on December 30, 2018.

Grâu, Lina, "Vybory parlamenta i Pridnestrov'e," Radio Europe Liberă Moldova, March 4, 2019. As of July 12, 2019:
https://moldova.europalibera.org/a/pridnestrovskie-dialoghi-/29831846.html

Hammarberg, Thomas, and Magdalena Grono, *Human Rights in Abkhazia Today*, Stockholm, Sweden: Olof Palme International Center, July 2017. As of July 12, 2019:
https://www.palmecenter.se/wp-content/uploads/2017/07/Human-Rights-in-Abkhazia-Today-report-by-Thomas-Hammarberg-and-Magdalena-Grono.pdf

Horowitz, Donald L., *A Democratic South Africa? Constitutional Engineering in a Divided Society*, Berkeley, Calif.: University of California Press, 1991.

International Crisis Group, *Abkhazia: Deepening Dependence*, Brussels, February 26, 2010a. As of July 12, 2019:
https://www.crisisgroup.org/europe-central-asia/caucasus/georgia/abkhazia-deepening-dependence

———, *South Ossetia: The Burden of Recognition*, Brussels, June 7, 2010b. As of July 12, 2019:
https://www.crisisgroup.org/europe-central-asia/caucasus/south-ossetia-burden-recognition

———, *Abkhazia and South Ossetia: Time to Talk Trade*, Brussels, Europe Report No. 249, May 24, 2018. As of July 12, 2019:
https://www.crisisgroup.org/europe-central-asia/caucasus/georgia/249-abkhazia-and-south-ossetia-time-talk-trade

International Institute for Strategic Studies, "Eurasia's Economic Bloc at Risk from Geopolitics," *Strategic Comments*, Vol. 21, No. 5, October 2015, pp. xi–xii.

Kanashvili, Giorgi, "He Who Says A Must Say B—or Why Tornike Sharashenidze's Abkhazia Policy Fails," *Civil Georgia*, October 13, 2017. As of July 12, 2019:
https://civil.ge/archives/218375

Kapanadze, Sergi, Ulrich Kühn, Wolfgang Richter, and Wolfgang Zellner, *Status-Neutral Security, Confidence-Building and Arms Control Measures in the Georgian Context*, Hamburg, Germany: Institute for Peace Research and Security Policy, CORE Working Paper No. 28, January 2017. As of July 12, 2019:
https://ifsh.de/file-CORE/documents/Working_Papers/CORE_WP28_en_.pdf

Ker-Lindsay, James, "The Policies of Greece and Cyprus Towards Turkey's EU Accession," *Turkish Studies*, Vol. 8, No. 1, 2007, pp. 71–83.

"Kishinev i Tiraspol' vozobnovili gruzovoe zheleznodorozhnoe soobshchenie cherez territoriyu Pridnestrov'ya, prervannoe 6 let nazad," *interlic*, April 26, 2012. As of July 12, 2019:
http://ru.interlic.md/2012-04-26/kishinev-i-tiraspol-vozobnovili-gruzovoe-zheleznodorozhnoe-soobcshenie-cherez-territoriju-pridnestro-24859.html

Kofner, Yuri, "Desyat' prichin, pochemu EAES i ES stoit sotrudnichat'," Valdai Club, June 26, 2019. As of August 28, 2019:
http://ru.valdaiclub.com/a/highlights/desyat-prichin-eaes-i-es/

Lehne, Stefan, *Reviving the OSCE: European Security and the Ukraine Crisis*, Washington, D.C.: Carnegie Endowment for International Peace, September 22, 2015. As of July 11, 2019:
https://carnegieeurope.eu/2015/09/22/reviving-osce-european-security-and-ukraine-crisis-pub-61362

"Lukashenko: Idea to Launch New International Negotiating Process Gains More Supporters," BelTA, October 31, 2018. As of September 4, 2019:
https://eng.belta.by/president/view/lukashenko-idea-to-launch-new-international-negotiating-process-gains-more-supporters-116189-2018/

Markedonov, Sergey, "A Post-Soviet Anomaly: How Karabakh Could Bring Russia and the West Together," Carnegie Moscow Center, October 10, 2017. As of July 12, 2019:
https://carnegie.ru/commentary/73335

Mazarr, Michael J., Miranda Priebe, Andrew Radin, and Astrid Stuth Cevallos, *Understanding the Current International Order*, Santa Monica, Calif.: RAND Corporation, RR-1598-OSD, 2016. As of September 4, 2019:
https://www.rand.org/pubs/research_reports/RR1598.html

Mearsheimer, John, "Why the Ukraine Crisis Is the West's Fault," *Foreign Affairs*, Vol. 93, No. 5, September/October 2014.

Menon, Rajan, and Jack L. Snyder, "Buffer Zones: Anachronism, Power Vacuum, or Confidence Builder?" *Review of International Studies*, Vol. 43, No. 5, December 2017, pp. 962–986.

Ministry of Defense of Moldova, "Peacekeeping Missions," webpage, undated. As of August 28, 2019:
https://www.army.md/?lng=3&action=show&cat=163

"Moldova ustanovila shest' migratsionnykh postov v Zone bezopasnosti na Dnestre," webpage, undated. As of August 28, 2019:
http://dniester.eu/813

Nantoi, Oazu, "Barter moldovenesc—suveranitatea declarata contra integritatii iluzorii," Institutul de Politici Publice, May 21, 2001. As of August 28, 2019:
http://ipp.md/old/print.php?l=ro&idc=154&id=399

Nanuashvili, Ucha, "Helping the Abkhaz, Ossetians Is Georgia's Obligation," *Civil Georgia*, November 20, 2017. As of July 12, 2019:
https://civil.ge/archives/218833

"Nazvana chislennost' naseleniya Pridnestrov'ya," *point*, March 1, 2017. As of July 12, 2019:
https://point.md/ru/novosti/obschestvo/nazvana-chislennost-naseleniia-pridnestrovia

Office of the State Minister of Georgia for Reconciliation and Civic Equality, *"A Step to a Better Future": Peace Initiative, Enhancing Educational Opportunities for the Residents of Abkhazia and Tskhinvali Region/South Ossetia*, Tbilisi, Georgia, 2018a. As of July 12, 2019:
http://smr.gov.ge/Uploads/Education__9dd0e9dc.pdf

———, *"A Step to a Better Future": Peace Initiative, Facilitation of Trade Across Dividing Line*, Tbilisi, Georgia, 2018b. As of July 12, 2019:
http://smr.gov.ge/Uploads/Concept_EN_0eaaac2e.pdf

Office of the State Minister for Reintegration of the Republic of Georgia, "Action Plan for Engagement," July 2010. As of July 12, 2019:
http://smr.gov.ge/Uploads/action_pla_3395c13d.pdf

Organization for Security and Co-operation in Europe, "OSCE Special Monitoring Mission to Ukraine," webpage, undated. As of July 12, 2019:
https://www.osce.org/special-monitoring-mission-to-ukraine

———, Vienna Document 2011: On Confidence- and Security-Building Measures, Vienna, November 30, 2011. As of September 16, 2019:
https://www.osce.org/fsc/86597?download=true

———, "Joint Statement by the Heads of Delegation of the OSCE Minsk Group Co-Chair Countries," December 4, 2014. As of July 12, 2019:
https://www.osce.org/mg/129421

———, "OSCE Mission to Moldova Welcomes Start of 'Licence Plate' Agreement Implementation by the Sides," September 1, 2018. As of July 12, 2019: https://www.osce.org/chairmanship/392231

OSCE—*See* Organization for Security and Co-operation in Europe.

Panel of Eminent Persons on European Security as a Common Project, *Back to Diplomacy*, Vienna: Organization for Security and Co-operation in Europe, 2015.

Parliament of Georgia, Law of Georgia on Occupied Territories, No. 431, October 23, 2008.

Parliament of the Republic of Moldova, Zakon Nr. 1024 ot 02.06.2000 o grazhdanstve Respubliki Moldova, August 10, 2000.

"Poezda iz Ukrainy v Moldovu opyat' poedut cherez Pridnestrov'e," *ZN*, January 14, 2011. As of July 12, 2019: https://zn.ua/ARCHIVE/poezda_iz_ukrainy_v_moldovu_opyat_poedut_cherez_pridnestrovie.html

Preiherman, Yauheni, "Belarus Finds Its Foreign Policy Stride," *Global Brief*, Fall/Winter 2019. As of July 11, 2019: http://minskdialogue.by/en/research/opinions/belarus-finds-its-foreign-policy-stride

President of Russia, "Deklaratsiya Prezidenta Rossiiskoi Federatsii, Prezidenta Ukrainy, Prezidenta Frantsuzskoi Respubliki i Kantslera Federativnoi Respubliki Germaniya v podderzhku Kompleksa mer po vypolneniyu Minskikh soglashenii," February 12, 2015. As of July 12, 2019: http://kremlin.ru/supplement/4803

Rainio-Niemi, Johanna, "Cold War Neutrality in Europe: Lessons to Be Learned?" in Heinz Gartner, ed., *Engaged Neutrality: An Evolved Approach to the Cold War*, Lanham, Md.: Lexington Books, 2017, pp. 15–36.

"Rossiya otpravila v Donbass novuyu kolonnu s gumanitarnoi pomoshch'yu," *RIA Novosti*, November 22, 2018. As of July 12, 2019: https://ria.ru/20181122/1533265662.html

"Russia Suspends Free Trade Agreement with Ukraine," *Moscow Times*, December 16, 2015. As of July 12, 2019: https://www.themoscowtimes.com/2015/12/16/russia-suspends-free-trade-agreement-with-ukraine-a51261

Sharashenidze, Tornike, "Why Georgia's Abkhazia Policy Has Failed," *Civil Georgia*, October 5, 2017. As of July 12, 2019: https://civil.ge/archives/218349

Shnirelman, V. A., *Voiny pamyati: Mify, identichnost' i politika v Zakavkaz'e*, Moscow: Nauka, 2003.

Shraibman, Artyom, "Belarus, the Tactical Peacemaker," Carnegie Moscow Center, June 25, 2018. As of July 11, 2019: https://carnegie.ru/commentary/76615

Sotieva, Larisa, Arda Inal-Ipa, Jana Javakhishvili, and Liana Kvarchelia, *Envisioning Peace: An Analysis of Grassroots Views on the Nagorny Karabakh Conflict*, London: International Alert, October 2018. As of July 12, 2019: https://www.international-alert.org/sites/default/files/Caucasus_EnvisioningPeace_EN_2018.pdf

"South Ossetia Becomes Thorn in Russia's Side," *Spiegel Online*, December 24, 2008. As of July 12, 2019: https://www.spiegel.de/international/world/six-months-after-caucasus-war-south-ossetia-becomes-thorn-in-russia-s-side-a-598311.html

Stiles, Kendall W., *Trust and Hedging in International Relations*, Ann Arbor, Mich.: University of Michigan Press, 2018.

Synoweic, Ewa, "The EU Is Encouraging Belarus to Join the World Trade Organisation," *Emerging Europe*, December 30, 2016. As of July 11, 2019: https://emerging-europe.com/voices/the-eu-is-encouraging-belarus-to-join-the-world-trade-organisation/

Tsvizhba, Asmat, "Kvota na mechty: Kak iz Abkhazii popast' v rossiiskii vuz," Sputnik, July 10, 2019. As of July 12, 2019: https://sputnik-abkhazia.ru/Abkhazia/20190710/1027870354/Kvota-mechty-kak-Abkhazii-popast-rossiyskiy-vuz.html

United Nations, "UN Comtrade Database," database, undated. As of September 9, 2017: https://comtrade.un.org/

———, Letter Dated 7 December 1994 from the Permanent Representatives of the Russian Federation, Ukraine, the United Kingdom of Great Britain and Northern Ireland and the United States of America to the United Nations Addressed to the Secretary-General, December 19, 1994. As of December 7, 2017: http://www.securitycouncilreport.org/atf/cf/%7B65BFCF9B-6D27-4E9C-8CD3-CF6E4FF96FF9%7D/s_1994_1399.pdf

Wilson, Damon, *Georgia's Path to NATO*, Washington, D.C.: Atlantic Council, February 2014. As of July 11, 2019: https://www.atlanticcouncil.org/wp-content/uploads/2014/02/Georgias_Path_to_NATO.pdf

WTO—*See* World Trade Organization.

World Trade Organization, "Accessions: Belarus," webpage, undated. As of July 12, 2019: https://www.wto.org/english/thewto_e/acc_e/a1_belarus_e.htm#status

Zellner, Wolfgang, Philip Remler, Wolfgang Richter, Andrei Zagorski, Evgeny P. Buzhinsky, Vladislav L. Chernov, Ali Serdar Erdurmaz, Marc Finaud, Cornelius Friesendorf, P. Terrence Hopmann, Lukasz Kelsa, Igors Rajevs, Benjamin Schaller, Hans-Joachim Schmidt, Niklas Schörnig, Oleg Shakirov, and Simon Weiß, *Reducing the Risks of Conventional Deterrence in Europe: Arms Control in the NATO-Russia Contact Zones*, Vienna: OSCE Network of Think Tanks and Academic Institutions, 2018. As of July 11, 2019: http://osce-network.net/file-OSCE-Network/Publications/RISK_SP.pdf

Zhidkov, S. K., *Brosok maloi imperii*, Maikop, Russia: Adygeya, 1996.

Author and Editor Biographies

Note: The authors take responsibility only for the chapter(s) to which they contributed.

Sergey Afontsev is deputy director of the Primakov National Research Institute of World Economy and International Relations of the Russian Academy of Sciences and a professor at the Moscow State Institute of International Relations (MGIMO).

Péter Balás is a senior policy adviser and member of the Covington law firm's Public Policy team. He has served as deputy director general, DG Trade to the European Commission (2005–2014) and head of the Support Group for Ukraine in the European Commission (2014–2015). He was previously ambassador and permanent representative of Hungary to the World Trade Organization. He also held several positions working for the Hungarian government, including as deputy state secretary for international economic relations at the Ministries of Economic Affairs (1996–2000) and Foreign Affairs (2000–2002), assistant state secretary in the Ministry of Industry and Trade (1994–1996), and director-general in the Ministry of International Economic Relations in Budapest (1991–1994).

Oleksandr Chalyi serves as the president of Grant Thornton, Ukraine, where he specializes in issues related to international and corporate law, particularly international agreements and contracts. Previously, he served as first deputy minister for foreign affairs of Ukraine, state secretary for European Integration, and foreign policy adviser to the President of Ukraine. He has headed Ukrainian delegations for World

Trade Organization membership negotiations, with international institutions like the World Bank group, the European Bank for Reconstruction and Development, and the European Investment Bank. In 2014, he was named a member of the Organization for Security and Co-operation in Europe's Eminent Persons Panel.

Samuel Charap is a senior political scientist at the RAND Corporation. His work focuses on the political economy and foreign policies of Russia and the former Soviet states; European and Eurasian regional security; and U.S.-Russia deterrence, strategic stability, and arms control. From November 2012 until April 2017, he was the senior fellow for Russia and Eurasia at the International Institute for Strategic Studies. Prior to joining the International Institute for Strategic Studies, he served at the U.S. Department of State as senior adviser to the undersecretary for arms control and international security and on the secretary's policy planning staff, covering Russia and Eurasia. He is the coauthor, with Timothy Colton, of *Everyone Loses: The Ukraine Crisis and the Ruinous Contest for Post-Soviet Eurasia* (Routledge, 2017). He holds a Ph.D. in political science and an M.Phil. in Russian and East European studies from the University of Oxford.

Rodica Crudu is dean of the International Economic Relations Faculty at the Academy of Economic Studies of Moldova (ASEM), where she has been a professor since 2004, and the deputy coordinator of the Jean Monnet Centre of Excellence in European Economic Integration Studies. Since 2014, she has held the title of Jean Monnet professor, coordinating several Jean Monnet projects in Moldova in the field of European integration studies. From August 2017 until January 2018, she held a Fulbright fellowship at American University in Washington, D.C. Her research interests include the economic aspects of European integration, innovation policies and entrepreneurship, international trade, trade policy, and European Union–Moldova trade relations. She holds a Ph.D. in international relations and affairs from ASEM.

Alexandra Dienes is a research associate at Friedrich Ebert Stiftung (FES)'s Regional Office for Cooperation and Peace in Europe, where she focuses on economic aspects of regional security and cooperation and coordinates the Fresh Look on Eastern European Trends network of young experts. Before joining FES in 2017, she taught international relations and political economy at the University of Amsterdam and interned for German political foundations in Georgia and China, the European Parliament in Brussels, and the German Development Agency. She holds an M.A. in political science from the Freie University Berlin and a Ph.D. from the University of Amsterdam.

James Dobbins is a senior fellow and distinguished chair in Diplomacy and Security at the RAND Corporation. He has held State Department and White House posts, including assistant secretary of state for Europe, special assistant to the President for the Western Hemisphere, special adviser to the President, secretary of state for the Balkans, and ambassador to the European Community. Ambassador Dobbins has served on numerous crisis-management and diplomatic troubleshooting assignments as special envoy for Afghanistan and Pakistan, Kosovo, Bosnia, Haiti, and Somalia for the administrations of Barack Obama, George W. Bush, and Bill Clinton. In 2013, he returned to the State Department to become the Obama administration's special representative for Afghanistan and Pakistan, returning to RAND in 2014.

John Drennan is a policy analyst at the RAND Corporation. Before joining RAND, he was special assistant to the executive director, IISS-Americas, at the International Institute for Strategic Studies. Prior to that, he was a research analyst and program officer in the Institute's Russia and Eurasia Program, where his research focused on Russian foreign and security policy, U.S.-Russia relations, and Central Asia. He holds an M.A. in strategic studies and international economics from the Johns Hopkins University School of Advanced International Studies and a B.A. in international studies, political science, and economics from Case Western Reserve University.

Vasyl Filipchuk is senior adviser at the International Center for Policy Studies in Kyiv. He has held numerous positions in the Ukrainian Ministry of Foreign Affairs, including as spokesman for the Foreign

Ministry, director of the Ministry's European Union Department, and director general of the Political and Security Department. In 2012 he chaired the European Integration Bureau under the aegis of Ukraine's cabinet of ministers. He is an expert on conflict resolution, peacebuilding, and nation-building processes in Central and Eastern Europe.

Diana Galoyan is vice-rector of academic affairs at the Armenian State University of Economics (ASUE), where she has taught since 2005. Prior to assuming the vice-rectorship, she served as head of ASUE's International Economic Relations Department. Since 2013, she has been a researcher at ASUE's AMBERD Research Center, one of Armenia's leading think tanks, focused on generating solutions to public policy and economic issues. She is the author of over 60 scientific publications, including ten monographs and five manuals.

Reinhard Krumm heads the regional office for Cooperation and Peace in Europe of the Friedrich Ebert Stiftung. He holds a doctorate from Regensburg University, Germany, where he has been a lecturer on Russian history since 2008. From 1991 to 1998, he was a journalist in the former Soviet Union, working as the Moscow correspondent of *Der Spiegel* from 1996 to 1998. He joined the Friedrich Ebert Stiftung in 2002, serving as the head of the Regional Central Asian office in Tashkent, Uzbekistan, from 2003 to 2007; the head of the Russian office in Moscow from 2007 to 2012; and the head of the Department of Central and Eastern Europe in Berlin from 2012 to 2016.

Ulrich Kühn is deputy head of the arms control and emerging technologies program at the Institute for Peace Research and Security Policy at the University of Hamburg and a nonresident scholar at the Carnegie Endowment for International Peace. Previously, he was a senior research associate at the Vienna Center for Disarmament and Non-Proliferation and a Stanton nuclear security fellow with Carnegie's nuclear policy program. His current research focuses on NATO-Russian relations, transatlantic security, nuclear and conventional deterrence and arms control, and the proceedings of the Organization for Security and Co-operation in Europe.

Yulia Nikitina is an associate professor of world politics and a research fellow at the Center for Post-Soviet Studies at the Moscow State Institute for International Affairs. She is a specialist on security in Eurasia with a focus on regional organizations. She is the author of the Russian-language book *The CSTO and SCO: Models of Security Regionalism* (2009) and of the textbook *Introduction to World Politics and International Relations* (2009).

Andrei Popov is president of the Moldovan Institute for Strategic Initiatives. He is the author of the weekly TV program, "Popular Diplomacy," and cohost of the weekly political talk show, "Botan+Popov." He is a former member of Parliament, deputy minister of foreign affairs and European Integration (2009–2013) and ambassador to Austria, Slovakia, and the Organization for Security and Co-operation in Europe in Vienna (2013–2016). He was executive director of the Foreign Policy Association of Moldova and is the founder of the Transnistrian Dialogues program. From 1997 to 2004, he served in the Moldovan diplomatic service. He is a John Smith and Munich Security Conference Young Leaders fellow.

Yauheni Preiherman is the founder and director of the Minsk Dialogue Council on International Relations. His main research interests include the foreign policies of small states, international affairs in Eastern Europe, and Euroatlantic and Eurasian security. Yauheni is a regular contributor to the *Eurasia Daily Monitor* of the Jamestown Foundation, *Global Brief*, and other Belarusian and international publications. His articles and comments have appeared in *Foreign Policy*, *Kommersant*, *Vedomosti*, and other publications.

Pernille Rieker is a research professor at the Norwegian Institute of International Affairs (NUPI) and coordinator of the NUPI Centre for European Studies. Her research focuses on European integration and European foreign and security policy. She has previously served as a senior researcher and head of the department for international politics at NUPI and an adviser to the Nordic Research Board. She holds a Ph.D. in political science from the University of Oslo.

Gwendolyn Sasse has been the director of the Centre for East European and International Studies since October 2016. She is professor of comparative politics at the Department of Politics and International Relations and at the School of Interdisciplinary Area Studies at the University of Oxford and is a professorial fellow at Nuffield College and nonresident senior fellow at Carnegie Europe. Her academic career spans the study of history, Slavonic studies, and political science at the University of Hamburg and an M.Sc. and Ph.D. in political science at the London School of Economics. After gaining her doctorate, she first took up a post as assistant professor at the Central European University, and then as lecturer/senior lecturer at the London School of Economics before moving to Oxford in 2007, where she became a full professor in 2013.

Jeremy Shapiro is research director at the European Council on Foreign Relations. Previously, he was a fellow in the Project on International Order and Strategy and the Center on the United States and Europe at the Brookings Institution, where he edited the foreign policy program's blog, *Order from Chaos*. Prior to Brookings, he was a member of the U.S. State Department's policy planning staff, where he advised the Secretary of State on U.S. policy in North Africa and the Levant. He was also the senior adviser to Assistant Secretary of State for European and Eurasian Affairs, Philip Gordon, providing strategic guidance on a wide variety of U.S.-European foreign policy issues.

Nikolai Silaev is a Russian political scientist and a specialist on regional conflicts. He is a graduate of the history faculty of Moscow State University and has a Ph.D. in history. He has been a senior research associate at the Center for Caucasian Studies and Regional Security of Moscow State Institute for International Affairs since 2004. He is director of Caucasian Cooperation, a nonprofit organization facilitating international connections within the Caucasus.

Olesya Vartanyan is the International Crisis Group's analyst for the European Union Eastern Neighbourhood. Based in Tbilisi, she researches regional security issues in Armenia, Georgia, and Azerbaijan, with a focus on breakaway regions in the South Caucasus: Abkhazia, Nagorno-Karabakh, and South Ossetia. Before joining the International Crisis Group, she worked as a journalist covering security and conflict-related issues in Georgia and its breakaway regions. With her field reporting during the 2008 Russia-Georgia war, Olesya contributed to groundbreaking investigations by the *New York Times* about the origins of the conflict. She has also covered this region for Radio Free Europe/Radio Liberty. In 2013, Olesya received the first EU Monitoring Mission special prize in Peace Journalism. She holds an M.A. in war studies from King's College London and an M.A. from the Georgian Institute of Public Affairs' Media School.

Andrei Zagorski is the director of the Department of Arms Control and Conflict Resolution Studies at the Primakov National Research Institute of World Economy and International Relations of the Russian Academy of Sciences and professor of international relations at Moscow State Institute for International Affairs. His work focuses on European security, relations between Russia and NATO, and relations between Russian and European organizations (the Organization for Security and Co-operation in Europe, the European Union, European Council). From 1981 to 1992, he was a full-time researcher at the Center for International Studies at MGIMO; from 1992 to 1999, he was a vice-rector at the same institution. From 1999 to 2000, he was a senior vice president of the EastWest Institute in Prague. In 2001, he served as director of the project "Networking of the Early Warning Systems," of the EastWest Institute. He has held his current position since 2011.

CPSIA information can be obtained
at www.ICGtesting.com
Printed in the USA
BVHW041046141119
563827BV00013B/261/P